Some highlighting $ 10
                                     10/18

D1539061

Business Process Management and the Balanced Scorecard

Business Process Management and the Balanced Scorecard

Using Processes as Strategic Drivers

Ralph F. Smith

John Wiley & Sons, Inc.

Published by John Wiley & Sons, Inc., Hoboken, New Jersey.

Published simultaneously in Canada.

For general information on our other products and services, or technical support, please contact our Customer Care Department within the United States at 800-762-2974, outside the United States at 317-572-3993 or fax 317-572-4002.

Wiley also publishes its books in a variety of electronic formats. Some content that appears in print may not be available in electronic books.

For more information about Wiley products, visit our Web site at http://www.wiley.com.

Library of Congress Cataloging-in-Publication Data

Smith, Ralph F., 1963-
  Business Process Management and the Balanced Scorecard : using processes as strategic drivers / Ralph F. Smith.
     p. cm.
  Includes index.
  ISBN-13: 978-0-470-04746-0 (cloth)
  ISBN-10: 0-470-04746-1 (cloth)
  1. Workflow--Management. 2. Benchmarking (Management) 3. Performance--Management. 4. Strategic planning. I. Title.
  HD62.17.S65 2007
  658.5'1--dc22

                       2006020850

Printed in the United States of America

10 9 8 7 6 5 4 3 2

To my loving wife Janet,
whose patience and support make everything possible.

CONTENTS

PREFACE

Why write a business book? Aren't there enough of them out there already? It's a great question. There are so many books, methodologies, and competing theories on how to be successful in today's business world that there doesn't seem to be a crying need for another one. I mulled this over for many an evening before committing the time and effort to produce this text. The factor that convinced me to proceed was recalling that most of the business books I have read tend to be theoretical, conceptual, and difficult to put into practice. My first thought when reading many of these texts is "sounds good—but how do I *do* it?"

My career has been spent helping organizations implement these big-picture ideas. I have been very successful over the years in translating theory into common sense terms so others can be comfortable with the how-to of implementation. I think creative ideas are wonderful, but they are even better when properly implemented. So this book has been written to provide some common sense thoughts and implementation tips for process management and the balanced scorecard. In my opinion, the single biggest opportunity for many companies in today's world is to understand and leverage this synergy between strategy and process.

I have spent the last 16 years in the consulting business. My career started as an internal consultant in the heyday of total quality management (TQM), and through the years that followed I have been involved with such methodologies as reengineering, self-directed work teams, benchmarking, facilitating high-performance teams, Hoshin planning, strategy mapping, and the balanced scorecard. I've been around long enough now to watch fads come and go, and I've worked with enough companies to understand what makes them successful (and what doesn't!). Hopefully this text will provide useful insights to managers who are interested in improving their organizations by focusing on the link between processes and strategy.

I'd like to thank the talented and creative managers at (among many others) XL Capital, Texas Children's Hospital, the Michigan Department of the Treasury and Department of Management and Budget, Alcoa, and Brown's Hill Farm. I have learned at least as much from them through the years as they have learned from me. I'd also like to thank original thinkers like Dr. Robert Kaplan, Dr. David Norton, and Michael Hammer for their contributions to the business world. Their grasp of the big picture is extraordinary. And last but not least, I'd like to thank my partners at the Orion Development Group: Paul King, Bob Boehringer, Susan Williams, and Mandy Dietz are all extraordinary people, and their drive and intelligence has always spurred me on to greater heights than I ever thought possible.

Enjoy the book! I hope you have as much fun reading it as I did in acquiring the experience to write it.

CHAPTER I

A WORLD OF CHANGE

What is the most important ingredient for the success of an organization?

If a typical executive is asked what makes his/her company great, the likely response will be one of the following:

"We are more profitable than our competitors"

"We have strong relationships with our customers"

"Our people are the best in the industry"

Very rarely will an executive lead off the discussion of greatness by describing process performance. Yet, ironically, process performance has become perhaps the most critical driver of organizational success in the 2000's. A high-performing organization in today's marketplace must not only understand how to identify and correct its process weaknesses (an age old practice), but it must also be able to leverage process strengths and opportunities for strategic advantage.

The fact that processes are so crucial to future success is an interesting phenomenon; analyzing and improving processes is definitely not a revolutionary concept. In fact, many of the tools and techniques (e.g., flowcharts, control charts) used for process improvement have been around for decades. Why, then, is the emphasis on process getting stronger and stronger? It is due to a combination of factors that have impacted the business world over the last several years. A basic change management principle holds that "things are the way they are because they got that way." This statement implies that it is critical to understand how a current situation developed and evolved if you truly want to be effective in changing the status quo. By taking a few snapshots of the business climate of the past and describing how certain trends have emerged, it will be possible to illustrate how and why process focus is so critical today. The comparisons will be of the business world in three time frames: 1970, 1985, and present day.

1970

Take a moment to think about the United States circa 1970. The median household income was around $8,700. Richard Nixon was President. Kansas City topped Minnesota 23–7 in Super Bowl IV. The Beatles broke up. Four students at Kent State University were killed by National Guardsmen. In the business world, the Big Three automobile manufacturers dominated the American market, posting a combined market share of over 90%. Gas was around 30 cents per gallon. IBM introduced the first floppy disk, and a newly formed company named Intel introduced a new generation of computer chips that quickly elevated the company to a market leader. AT&T held a monopoly in the telephone industry. And you could buy a hamburger, french fries, and drink at McDonald's for around $1.

The business environment was completely different than what we are familiar with today. For example, consider the nature and composition of the workforce. In 1970 employees weren't nearly as mobile; entire careers were often spent with the same company. (In fact, the perception of someone who moved from company to company as a chosen career path was very negative.) Because changing jobs was so rare, it follows that the 1970s was an environment of heavy seniority. Process knowledge was carried around in the heads of employees, and when people retired, they passed their knowledge on to their successors. Employees were expected to be able to rely on their extensive experience within the organization to work around process difficulties as they emerged. Managers were typically selected from within and promoted up through the chain of command, so by the time an employee reached executive level, he or she had a firm grasp of the process complexities of the organization. (Of course, this was only effective if the employee in question was rotated around the organization as he or she was promoted over the course of time. Managers who had always been part of the sales chain-of-command, for example, were sometimes crowned CEO or COO and had no real experience with any of the nonsales aspects of the organization. In this case the advantage of having years of experience with the company was somewhat minimized.)

Processes were different in this era as well. It was still the age of specialization. The majority of organizations had the vertical type of organizational structure depicted in Exhibit 1.1.

The basis for this type of structure was rooted in the division of labor concepts dating back to Adam Smith in the 1700s. Each person on the lower levels was responsible for one specific task, the job of the first-line manager was to make sure these tasks were performed properly, the next-level managers made sure that the first-line managers performed their tasks properly, and so on up the ranks.

EXHIBIT 1.1 *Vertical Organizational Structure*

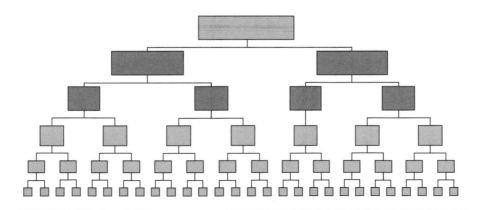

Some degree of specialization is undoubtedly necessary in any organization to ensure needed expertise is present, but this type of organizational structure can have profoundly negative effects on processes. Any process that requires even a moderate degree of cross-functional cooperation is bound to be handicapped by this type of structure. At the lowest levels, each link in the chain will only be looking out for and trying to optimize a *portion* of the process as opposed to the *entire* process. Because many companies during this era rewarded their employees based on how well they performed with regard to their own specific area, this created some very interesting behavior.

For example, a major aluminum manufacturer once paid its employees by the pound of material produced per hour. This reinforced the behavior that the heavier the job, the more important it must be. It also reinforced the behavior that changeovers and new setups were bad, so big jobs must be more important than small jobs. The employees in this department therefore paid little attention to customer needs, job due dates, or special requests from other departments. In fact, they often ran material that wasn't even needed and stored it in inventory in order to artificially inflate their pounds-per-hour number. Because inventory management was someone else's worry, these employees saw no negatives to this type of behavior. The paint line in this same company was paid by how many pieces they painted. There were instances when no material was ready to be painted, so they retrieved material out of the scrap heap, painted it, and threw it back on the scrap heap just to make their numbers look good. This type of behavior obviously came at a cost to the company, but in the environment of 1970 it was possible to simply pass the added cost on to the customer with minimal effect on the organization.

In addition to reinforcing counterproductive behaviors, this specialized and hierarchical organizational structure made internal communication extremely difficult. Creating silos within the company hampered cross-functional information sharing. When Chrysler wanted to develop a new model car, its process cycle time (measured from idea-to-showroom-floor) was five years. This obviously implied enormous risk, since the market and consumer preferences could change so much over a five-year period that by the time the new model was ready, it could be obsolete. The year 1970 was actually a prime example of this; most automobiles of this era were gas-guzzling behemoths with V8 engines. Any new vehicle beginning development in 1970 faced serious sales challenges in light of the impending energy crises of the early 1970s that shifted the focus to smaller, lighter cars (offered by the Japanese) that got better gas mileage.

And why did the process take five years? Because the practice was for each department to work on their portion of the process and then pass it on to the next department. There would then typically be a (sometimes large) time lag before the next department began processing its portion of the work, adding to the cycle time. And when the next department did begin its portion of the process, they often had to send things back to the first department, requesting changes, explanations, modifications, and so on. This would inject enormous amounts of lag time and rework into the process to no purpose. (*Note:* Chrysler recognized these shortcomings upon its purchase of American Motors Corporation and was able to reduce the idea-to-showroom-floor cycle time down to two years. This case will be examined in greater detail in subsequent chapters.) Because the U.S. economy had been so strong for so long, it was obvious that this type of process inefficiency had been camouflaged, with no real repercussions.

Another reason for process and internal communication difficulties was the lack of communication technology. There were no cell phones, e-mail systems, wireless networks, or Internet in 1970, making communication much more difficult than it is today. This phenomenon not only slowed down internal processes and knowledge sharing, but it had a significant effect on the marketplace in general as well. Lack of communication technology meant that in many cases the competition a typical company faced was more local in nature versus the global competition seen today. Therefore, the customer didn't have as many choices, and many companies didn't have the sense of urgency to improve. The local companies typically weren't capitalized like global companies of today are, limiting their ability to employ different pricing and promotional strategies.

It was only possible for companies to thrive in this environment because customer expectations were also very different in 1970. It was common for an automobile manufacturer to sell a new car to a customer and say, "Make a list of all the problems you find and bring the vehicle back in a month and we'll fix all of them." The customer didn't even have a "take it or leave it" option; the situation was "take it or take it!" In this environment all manner of process problems could be masked by price increases and the "find it and fix it" mentality. Process and the resultant product quality were low and prices were relatively high, but demand for products and services made everything appear all right. The auto industry is referenced throughout this text simply because for many decades it served as the backbone of the American economy and was the first to face extended and intense competition from global sources, which began shortly after the 1970 reference date. (Honda introduced the first Civic to the United States in 1972, ushering in the new age of global competition.)

1985

Flash forward to 1985. The median household income was around $23,618, more than double what it was in 1970, although the cost of living more than kept pace with a 277% increase. Ronald Reagan was President, and Mikhail Gorbachev took over as leader of the Soviet Union. Madonna toured for the first time. Joe Montana and the San Francisco 49er's pounded Miami 38–16 in the Super Bowl. Scientists discovered a huge hole in the ozone over Antarctica. In the business world, Coca-Cola introduced New Coke and then quickly reintroduced Classic Coke. Relatively inexpensive laser printers and computers made desktop publishing commonplace. The first mobile phone call was made in Great Britain. Microsoft introduced the first version of Windows, appropriately numbered 1.0. Global competition was transforming many industries, headed by the Big Three losing their stranglehold on the auto market. (GM lost nearly one-third of its market share to overseas competitors between 1970 and 1985.)

Practically every factor mentioned in the 1970 discussion was subject to significant change by 1985. The intensity and quality of foreign competition forced American companies to reevaluate the way business was conducted and sparked an interest in total quality management (TQM). If applied properly, the basic tenets of TQM (e.g., good processes *reduce* cost versus adding cost, customer focus, measurement, worker involvement in improving their own jobs) addressed most of the problems exposed in the 1970s way of doing business. For example, consider the principle that worker input was important to both improving process performance and making the employee feel like a valued part of the organization. This became critical in the 1980s in light of the fact that the workforce was becoming more mobile. Many U.S. manufacturing jobs were being lost to international competition and being replaced by service industry jobs. The nature of the work required was more cerebral than physical, and the employees filling the positions saw no need to be loyal to a company that didn't value them or their ideas. Changing jobs no longer carried a negative stigma, which forced organizations to reevaluate their hiring practices, promotion policy, and factors leading to turnover of key employees.

Process analysis and improvement also underwent significant change in the mid-1980s. TQM begat cross-functional teams designed to improve communication and process performance across departmental lines. This was a major step forward, because it was the first attempt in many organizations to break free of the functional straightjacket in which their processes had been imprisoned for so many years. Flowcharts and process maps, which were not new tools even then, regained their importance. An executive with the aforementioned aluminum company commented that, "We found flowcharts that documented all of our processes and how they should work, and they were all dated from the late 1960s. It wasn't that we didn't know how to do this stuff. The problem was that things were going so well we felt we didn't need to pay close attention to process performance and documentation, so we fell asleep." The first wave of process improvement activities focused mainly on patching the holes in processes that had gradually become more and more broken over the years. This type of improvement strategy was known as *continuous improvement* and can be compared to taking a wrinkled shirt and ironing it so it is usable again. In other words, take the process and iron out the rough spots so it runs the way it was originally designed to run.

Technology also played a major role in the transformation of business in the mid-1980s, and this went hand-in-hand with process performance. Automation of sound processes enabled an organization to make major gains in operational performance, but automation of bad processes simply gave companies the capability to make bad products and deliver bad service faster. This was a painful lesson for one of the Big Three, as it spent literally tens of billions of dollars on automation in the decade leading up to 1985 and didn't get anywhere near the projected return on investment.

Customer needs and expectations also underwent dramatic change during this time frame. Customers were now inundated with products and services from a bigger range of competitors. In fact, international competition began to dominate entire industries. Many long-standing practices were eliminated practically overnight. Quality was higher and price was relatively lower than what customers were used to, and it was easy for them to adjust. Customers expected products to work right the first time; there was no interest in taking cars back to the dealer to get problems fixed or returning clothing to the store to get buttons sewn back on. Companies in many industries were forced to become more focused on maintaining strong customer relationships, as customers had more options to select from.

MID-2000S

The world in the mid-2000s has again undergone radical transformation. Global competition is now the norm. The Big Three automakers' market share has dropped below 60%, with over 30% now being held by Asian companies. Gas costs more than $2 per gallon. Mergers and acquisitions have been the order of the day in many industries, creating fewer, larger, and better capitalized companies. The Internet has completely changed the way business is transacted, because companies can access customers globally with minimal cost. The workforce has become even more mobile in terms of company-to-company movement. The heavy seniority, lifetime career approach of the 1970s has been turned upside down; in today's business environment, it seems that staying with a company too long could even be seen as a sign of stagnation. Customers are ever more demanding; the product and service features that were considered extravagant yesterday are standard expectations today. Advances in technology make the speed of conducting business increase faster and faster. The Big Blue of IBM has been challenged by the Big Green of Microsoft. The technology theme in the 1980s was about how much power could be brought to the desktop, while in the 2000s the theme has shifted to mobility and access to information from anywhere. Versatility of products is the order of the day. For example, it is now commonplace to have telephones that can send e-mails, take pictures, serve as stopwatches, and more.

HISTORICAL TREND IMPACT ON PROCESSES

All of these trends have a profound effect on the importance of having good processes. For example, consider the ever-increasing mobility of the workforce. In the 1970s companies could get away with letting their experienced employees carry all of the process knowledge around in their heads, without a lot of documentation. After all, people were in the same position for 30 years. All that was needed was to bring in a replacement a few months before the stalwart's impending retirement, have them teach the new person the ropes, and have the new person do the job for the next 30 years. This practice cannot be followed if positions turn over every few years, as is so common today. If an organization lets its process knowledge leave every 18 months, it is constantly putting itself in a position of starting from scratch. Well-documented processes are a must to keep the organization running smoothly.

Consider the example of McDonald's. Certainly they experience heavy turnover, as many of their employees are school-age people working for a short time by design and preference. Yet few organizations do a better job of ensuring process consistency. The french fries made by the McDonald's in New York or London or Tokyo or Sydney will be made using a consistent process and will taste basically the same. The customer never has any question what to expect when placing an order, and the resultant food quality will always meet the customers' preset expectations. While many organizations have processes that are more cross-functional and complicated than preparing hamburgers, the critical principle remains: processes must be documented and followed to ensure consistency in the face of a constantly changing workforce.

Mobility of the management team can also be a significant process inhibitor in today's business culture. In the 1970s a senior executive likely had many years of experience with the organization before assuming command. With all the job-hopping and external hiring done in the 2000s, it is common for executives to be unfamiliar with the customers, workers, and processes of the organization they have been hired to run. There is no doubt that learning about the customers and the employees takes a certain amount of time, but the technical details and experience required to truly understand organizational processes can take years. While it isn't necessary for executives to understand the complexities of every process, they do need to be familiar enough with the inner workings of the company to make proper resource allocation and strategic decisions. Many executives don't have the time, expertise, or interest to acquire the needed process knowledge, putting their company at a (sometimes significant) competitive disadvantage.

Telecommuting can present significant challenges to process performance as well. The concept of process improvement has always involved teams of people involved in analyzing and agreeing on how to change their process for the better. The whole sense of teamwork and camaraderie is more difficult to generate when parties are working remotely. It also increases the degree of difficulty of ensuring process consistency when it is more difficult to access, measure, and monitor process participants. In this environment it is essential to have well-documented processes and to train people in how to use them as they are introduced to their responsibilities.

Process excellence is also a key to leveraging the possibilities brought on by new distribution mechanisms. Pick, pack, and ship efficiency can drive significant profits through Internet sales. Cooperation with suppliers can also yield distribution efficiencies through technology. Consider the example of Wal-Mart: The merchandising giant has relationships with key suppliers in which they guarantee a certain amount of shelf space under the condition that the supplier keeps the shelves full of merchandise. This could not work efficiently without cooperation from both parties—and some slick technology. Like most stores, Wal-Mart electronically scans products at the checkout stand to determine how much to charge. What differentiates Wal-Mart from many other chains is that this information is instantly transmitted to its suppliers to inform them that product has been purchased. In this manner the supplier can keep a running total of inventory in each one of the stores and knows when it is time for replenishment. This is truly a win-win-win situation. The supplier wins because it gets premium shelf space and doesn't have to stock lots of excess inventory at each one of the stores. Wal-Mart wins because it avoids millions of dollars in inventory carrying costs. And the customer wins because some of the savings can be passed on in the form of lower prices.

The final trend referenced throughout this chapter that reinforces the importance of process is ever-increasing customer expectations. There is a constant drive in today's world to do it faster, better, and cheaper. Process excellence is often the only option available to meet customer needs. Because customer expectations are not likely to stop increasing in the future, process performance will be even more critical to meeting customer needs as time passes.

A summary of the evolution of business trends is presented in Exhibit 1.2.

EXHIBIT 1.2   *Business Trends Over Time*

Topic	1970	1985	2005	Impact on Processes
Competition	Local/regional Smaller competitors	National/ becoming global	Global Larger competitors	Must have processes capable of standing up to the best, well-capitalized companies in the world
Customers	Take whatever you give them Limited choices Prefer "made in the USA"	Standards increasing Demand higher quality products and services	Very demanding Loyal to whoever is currently the best	Processes must be able to deliver excellent quality at efficient quality at efficient prices just to meet customer needs
Processes	Functional focus Heavily manual	Recognizing need to integrate automation TQM generates focus on process improvement	Processes seen as enablers Cross-functional focus Technology-driven	Companies recognize there are many problems that cannot be solved functionally
Technology	Mainframes Focus on power	Desktops Focus on speed	Mobility Focus on access	An enabler only if processes are flowing smoothly to begin with
Workforce	Stable, with long term employees Experts on narrow range of tasks	Dynamic Increasing diversity Increasing breadth of knowledge needed	Mobile and diverse Premium on thinking versus simply doing Telecommuting/ working remotely	Processes must be well-documented to avoid losing institutional knowledge whenever an employee leaves

Companies that want to succeed in the business world of today must be prepared to face the new realities. Customers want results, the workforce wants a challenging and rewarding job experience, competition is tougher than ever before, and technology is providing unprecedented opportunities to explode forward. There is no question that success in this environment is possible only if an organization is ready to focus on using their processes as a strategic weapon to deliver world-class performance.

CHAPTER 2

HOW PROCESS CAN DRIVE STRATEGY

As the need for organizations to focus on processes has grown, so has the level of integration of process with the planning side of the organization (both strategic and operational planning). The manner in which organizations have improved and leveraged process performance has evolved through four stages over the years. These are shown in Exhibit 2.1.

THE FIRST WAVE: TOTAL QUALITY MANAGEMENT

As referenced in Chapter 1, total quality management (TQM) was a term that became popular in the mid-1980s. It was generally thought that the term originated with the Department of the Navy when it was trying to spread successful application of a set of principles in one location to multiple locations. A formal definition of the term comes from the Japanese Union of Scientists and Engineers (JUSE). They state that:

> TQM is a set of systematic activities carried out by the entire organization to effectively and efficiently achieve company objectives so as to provide products and services with a level of quality that satisfies customers, at the appropriate time and price.

> © 1998 The Deming Prize Application

EXHIBIT 2.1   *The Four Waves of Business Process Management*

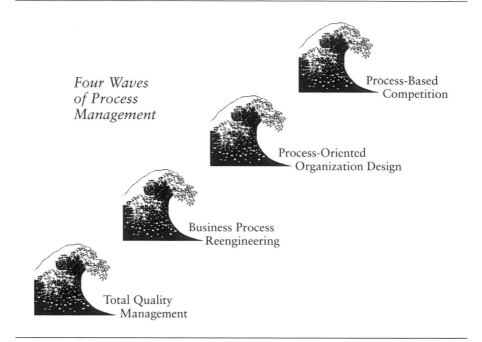

*Four Waves
of Process
Management*

Process-Based
Competition

Process-Oriented
Organization Design

Business Process
Reengineering

Total Quality
Management

There are several key parts of this definition. The first is that TQM was systematic. It involved applying the concepts of *continuous improvement* (referenced in Chapter 1) throughout the organization. The tools and techniques of TQM were both qualitative and quantitative. The statistical methods for evaluating data (statistical process control, or SPC) were a key component of the system, as were the process mapping and analysis tools such as flowcharts, cause-and-effect diagrams, and so on. The tools were used in the context of PDCA (Plan-Do-Check-Act, sometimes also referred to as PDSA, or Plan-Do-Study-Act). The *planning* portion of the methodology held that analysis of certain processes should be performed, data collected, and theories advanced regarding what needed to be changed to deliver improved process performance. The *do* involved actually implementing the identified process change. The *check* or *study* component required evaluation of the change to determine whether it was successful and should be continued, modified, or rejected, and based on this analysis the team or company would *act*. Instilling the PDCA mind-set in the workforce led to more efficient and effective processes; teams would constantly discover the problems in the processes within their functional area and find ways to solve them.

Successfully instilling this mindset into the workforce, however, could not be done without serious support from the management team. This is why the TQM definition stated that the entire organization had to be involved and that the goal was to achieve company objectives. Assigning employees the task of improving their processes required the cooperation and support of management, because process improvement does not come cheap. Management had to be willing not only to allocate resources to support process improvement ideas, but also to carve time out of the work schedule for employees and teams to focus on improvement. This was almost countercultural at the time, at least in the United States. The prior focus of "get it done and out the door as fast as you can" was replaced by "get it done properly so we don't have to do it again later."

A third key component of the definition was the customer satisfaction piece. TQM forced companies to think about customers instead of getting too absorbed with meeting internal targets. And the final statement regarding delivering at the appropriate time and price reinforces the notion that the definition of quality was total and process-focused. It would be impossible to deliver quickly, cheaply, and up to customer standards without strong process performance.

A typical TQM team would be assigned a problem, such as how to improve the yield on a certain production line. They would analyze the process and determine that the old machine routinely leaked oil on the pieces as they went by, and this was causing a 6% loss in productivity. The team would investigate the causes of the oil leak and further recognize that it wasn't the machine, but rather the faulty maintenance practices regarding the machine's upkeep. They would alter the practices, teach the maintenance people the new methods, and then collect data to substantiate that the 6% productivity gain was in fact realized. They would then put in place whatever safeguards were necessary to ensure that the new level would be maintained, and then they would disband.

This process was typically very formal at first. In other words, teams had to be approved by a management group, their progress carefully monitored by a facilitator, and their results documented for all to see. If the organization continued with TQM implementation over a number of years, the structure would gradually become unnecessary. Employees and teams would naturally be expected to think about process and solve problems using the methodology, without the need for so much formal supervision.

TQM was a popular methodology for several years, but unfortunately it was not always successful. There were multiple reasons for this, including but not limited to the following: (1) the initial structure needed to support the methodology was often too expensive and complicated to justify; (2) application of the statistical tools to non-manufacturing applications wasn't properly implemented; (3) lack of process knowledge contributed to selecting inappropriate topics for teams; and (4) poor relationships between management and nonmanagement stifled interest in team participation. The list is long, but the most relevant issue to the process wave was this: TQM wasn't set up to deliver order-of-magnitude types of improvement. To borrow a baseball analogy, the focus was on hitting singles versus hitting a home run. Changes that patched holes in existing processes were nice, but the speed of business was accelerating so rapidly that it became clear that a more aggressive type of process improvement would be needed.

THE SECOND WAVE: BUSINESS PROCESS REENGINEERING

Reengineering burst onto the scene in the early 1990s, popularized in the book *Reengineering the Corporation*, by Michael Hammer and James Champy. The focus of reengineering was dramatic and radical process redesign. It was the home run methodology many organizations with legacy process problems were looking for. To continue the analogy from the first chapter: *continuous improvement* meant ironing the wrinkles out of the shirt. *Reengineering* said the shirt is still four sizes too small, so ironing the wrinkles out won't help—you need to get a new one. Reengineering was therefore a much more aggressive approach, reasoning that the process wouldn't perform at an acceptable level even if all the wrinkles were gone. So reengineering was about starting with a blank sheet of paper and drawing up the perfect process, without regard to incumbent organizational barriers. This was a very exciting prospect to management team members who were charged with making significant strides quickly, so interest in the methodology blossomed rapidly.

Reengineering was a higher-risk, higher-reward proposition than TQM. The processes in question were typically larger, cross-functional, and of higher visibility within the organization. This meant that successful dramatic redesign would be of immense value to the company, but the obstacles to successfully doing it were also immense. The cross-functional nature of the process to be redesigned almost always meant that some departments would be seen as winners when a process was redesigned and others would be seen as losers. Managing the perceived losers represented a large behavioral challenge for the management team. The skills needed by the workforce to be successful in a reengineered process were often quite different than what the existing workforce was good at. This meant that success would not be possible without managing the workforce's fear of change and preparing them to succeed in their new roles.

While these were certainly not the only barriers, it is significant that the issues referenced previously were all behavioral in nature. It became apparent early in the reengineering years that technical solutions to technical problems were relatively easy to develop and implement. It was the challenge of dealing with change that often caused reengineering to fail. It has been estimated that 80% of the reengineering efforts that failed were caused by the inability to address the social issues.

A typical reengineering team would be formed to analyze not only a process but the surrounding stakeholders as well. If the process to be reengineered was product development, the team might include representatives from the departments responsible for current execution as well as IT, HR, customers, suppliers—anyone with a stake in the process might be eligible. The thought process of quantifying the current situation, making changes, and measuring improvement was similar to TQM, but the development of solutions followed a much different path. Instead of mapping out the existing process and looking for trouble spots, the team might take out a blank flipchart page and simply map out what the necessary functions of the process were. Product development might be summarized as shown in Exhibit 2.2.

This flow does not take the current process into account; there is no mention of who does what nor how they do it. The purpose of this diagram is to note the essential tasks and then determine potential new methods for performing them. For example, the research process might currently be done by the person who generated the idea. This could be changed in many ways. A formal research and development department could be formed, research could be outsourced, research for certain products could be deemed unnecessary, and so on. Everything is fair game when trying to find a reengineering type of solution. After proposing the new methods, the preferred option is selected and implementation begins.

Reengineering unfairly became a euphemism for downsizing in many organizations. The word was trendy, so whenever a company had layoffs it would claim it was because they had become more efficient and label it reengineering. Because of this there was often a negative stigma attached to the word, but many organizations were able to produce dramatic results by applying the concepts. For example, IBM Credit had a process that involved roughly a half-dozen departments and took over a week—simply to tell a customer whether they would approve financing for the mainframe computer they had already decided to buy.[1] A quick overview

EXHIBIT 2.2   *Product Development Process: Main Steps*

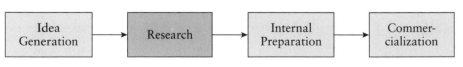

1. Reengineering the Corporation Michael Hammer and James Champy. Harper Collins, 1993.

of the process revealed that only about two hours of work was actually being performed throughout the entire process, and the rest of the time the multiple departments were simply passing the application back and forth.

The cross-functional solution was to break down the departmental walls and train everybody how to execute the entire process. Instead of having many people perform small and separate individual tasks, one person would work the application all the way through. The cycle time shrank from over a week down to just a few hours, delivering the order-of-magnitude reengineering-style improvement. Note that this problem could not have been resolved by a functional TQM team. The focus of the functional team would have been on the processing time of two hours, not the cycle time of over a week. Even cutting the processing time in half would not have had a significant impact on the overall cycle time. And the new process did not necessarily require fewer people, because the tasks being performed were virtually identical to what had been done previously. The difference was that most of the delay time for handoffs had been removed from the process.

Solutions like this one were widespread enough that many organizations realized there were huge gains to be made through focusing on process. But sometimes the cross-functional nature of reengineering improvements caused stress on the current functionally oriented organizational structure. In many organizations this caused a barrier that would force them to rethink how they were set up.

THE THIRD WAVE: PROCESS-ORIENTED ORGANIZATIONAL DESIGN

The IBM Credit example is an excellent illustration of the complexities that large-scale process redesign can impose on an organization. The solution sounds simple: just train everyone in six different departments to execute the entire process from beginning to end. Great idea, but what are the job descriptions for the new roles, who do the people report to, should a new department be created?—the list of organizational issues is long. This type of problem was the genesis for the third wave of process management, known as *process-oriented organizational design*. The purpose of the third wave is to set up an organizational structure that enhances the focus on process. This enables the key business processes within the organization to operate at maximum efficiency, delivering value both internally and to customers.

The trick when designing an organizational structure around processes is not to lose the functional benefits completely; there needs to be a balance between the two. Just like a heavily functional organization can suffer from process inefficiency, a totally process-oriented organization can suffer from lack of functional expertise. An interesting example of a process-oriented design comes from the State of Michigan Office of Retirement Services (ORS).

ORS was faced with significant challenges in the late 1990s and early 2000s. Impending retirement of the baby boomers threatened to overload processes that were already being stressed to their breaking point. Because the organization didn't expect to have the opportunity to increase staff to handle the additional workload, its only real option was to improve process efficiency. Several reengineering projects got things off to a good start, and then they redesigned the organization to fit the model in Exhibit 2.3.

The top of the diagram lists the Executive Director and his direct reports, just like any other traditional organizational structure. In this case the reporting functions were HR and Finance, Operations, Customer Service, and IT/Reengineering. Each of these functional areas had a director, middle management, front-line management, and employees. Reporting relationships were vertical/traditional, so ORS retained its emphasis on functional expertise.

What makes this example nontraditional is the process component illustrated on the left-hand side of the diagram. There were several groups of cross-functional processes, shown in the diagram as flowing from left to right. The organization created the titles of Business Process Executive (BPE) and Business Process Owner (BPO) to ensure that the core processes got the attention they needed as well. A BPO was someone

EXHIBIT 2.3   *Office of Retirement Services Process-Oriented Organizational Design*

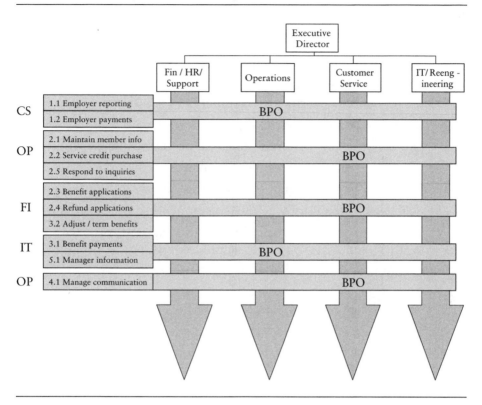

with broad subject matter expertise who was responsible for delivering process results. A BPE was a member of the executive team who did not have a direct link to the process. In other words, their function was not part of process execution. The BPE's responsibilities were to ensure that necessary cooperation and collaboration between functions happened so the overall process performance would not suffer.

For example, processes 1.1 Employee Reporting and 1.2 Employer Payments were closely related. Each is a core process rooted in operations. Therefore, the BPO title is listed under the Operations functional area, to note that the role is seated here. On the far left-hand side of the structure are the letters CS. This is to illustrate that the Director of Customer Service is the BPE for this group of processes. Because employee reporting and employer payments do not touch customer service, this manager will not be tempted to play favorites when overseeing process performance; the BPE can look out for the good of the process as opposed to worry about the impact on his or her own function. This setup also forces the management team to learn about processes from other parts of the organization, contributing to their ability to make better management decisions for the organization overall.

The end result of the ORS redesign was properly aligned leadership and employees, clear accountability for meeting customer needs, and dramatic process improvements such as those shown in Exhibit 2.4.

The challenge of the third wave was documenting the benefits of the redefined organizational structure. In the ORS example, processes were being reengineered as the structure was redesigned and implemented. Skeptics could claim that the impressive results were generated by

EXHIBIT 2.4   *ORS Process: Structure Redesign Results*

Measure	*1997*	*May 2005*
1st pension payment on effective date	Up to 6 months	98.3% in 60 days
Health insurance initiated on effective date	Up to 3 months	96.39% of the time
Telephone response rate— resolution on first contact	Inconsistent	93.2% of the time
Customer Satisfaction • Active • Retired	No records available 4 of 4 100%	77.5%
Written response rate (Up to a year)	Inconsistent in 10 days	Correspondence 99.5%
Employee Satisfaction	No records available	92.6%

process redesign and would have occurred regardless of organizational structure changes. Because the challenges of changing a structure were so formidable, many management teams determined that it wasn't worth the risk. While this reluctance to modify the structure to fit new processes surely caused *some* reengineering efforts to fail, the *precise* number of efforts failing because of ill-matched structure and process is unknown and unknowable.

The significance of the third wave, however, was that more and more companies started to realize that process performance was a key factor in their high-level decision making. Gone were the days when an executive team could simply look at financial reports to determine how the organization was performing. Process thinking had to be integrated into all management decisions, up to and including the structure of the organization. The final frontier was planning for the future of the organization by proactively leveraging process performance.

THE FOURTH WAVE: PROCESS-BASED COMPETITION

The fourth wave is where process performance is integrated into strategy. This means not only identifying the process weaknesses that have the most strategic significance and fixing them, but also understanding how process strengths can be better leveraged. The traditional strategic process in many organizations followed the thought process illustrated in Exhibit 2.5.

The links described in the diagram illustrate the traditional view of strategy. It was customary for the leaders of the organization to develop a strategic plan that would include a host of improvement initiatives. Some of these would inevitably be process improvement–type projects, whether of a continuous improvement or reengineering nature. Process improvement teams would then analyze the situation and develop new process innovations to help the organization run better, and these innovations would be integrated into the processes. But the fourth-wave picture is a bit different. It adds the link shown in Exhibit 2.6.

EXHIBIT 2.5   *The Strategy-Process Link*

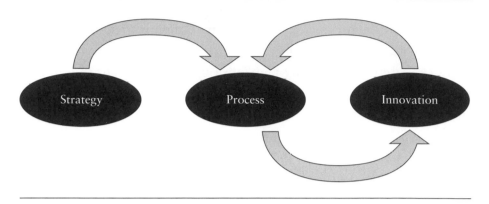

EXHIBIT 2.6   *The Process-Strategy Link*

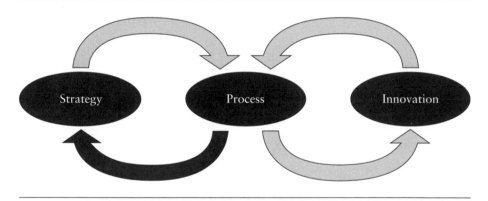

The dark arrow illustrates that in the fourth wave, process can be used to drive strategy. In other words, superior process performance could drive the future of the organization, helping capture new customers and markets, establishing additional profit centers, enabling the organization to provide more complete solutions by controlling more links in the value chain, and so forth. Fourth-wave companies are uniquely positioned to control their own destiny.

The next chapter introduces the strategic assessment process. The questions asked and techniques described within the process-focused assessment are designed to promote fourth-wave thinking. Examples of companies that have flourished will be provided in the context of illustrating how the assessment tools can work.

CHAPTER 3

THE STRATEGIC PROCESS

Chapter 2 presented the premise that organizations can leverage process performance for strategic gain. This chapter provides an overview and explanation of the strategic process, building a bridge to the discussion of how to develop a proper strategy that leverages process performance.

THE STRATEGIC PROCESS FLOWCHART

There are dozens of ways to approach the development of strategy. While on a detail level there can be significant differences, most methods focus on a flow of steps as shown in Exhibit 3.1.

Each step will be examined, and a brief explanation of what it is about and why it is part of the process will be provided.

VISION AND MISSION

The *vision and mission* step is one of the most important and least understood. Referencing five different books on strategic planning can commonly yield five different explanations of what mission and vision statements are and what they are supposed to accomplish. (A scary proposition since it implies that the writers, who are supposedly experts

EXHIBIT 3.1   *The Strategic Process*

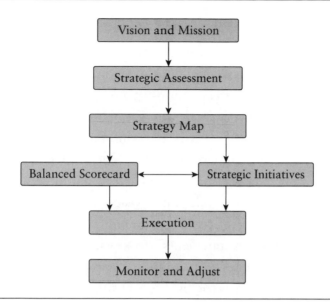

on the subject, cannot even agree!) Simple user-friendly definitions are as follows:

- A **vision statement** should articulate the ideal future state of the organization. In other words, if you are successful in driving the organization in the desired direction, what will it look like when you get there?
- A **mission statement** describes what the organization is in business to do.

The purpose and value of the vision statement is literally to ensure that everyone (particularly the leaders) in an organization has the same view of what they want the future to look like. In the movie *Forrest Gump*, the lead character said, "If you don't know where you are going, you're probably not gonna get there." This is a perfect and straightforward way to think about why an organization needs a vision.

The purpose of the mission is simply to provide focus for current decision making and the resulting resource allocation. In other words, if an opportunity requires capital and supports what the organization is in business to do, it should be strongly considered. But if an opportunity requires capital and *doesn't* support the mission, it should be weighed accordingly. The value of the mission is therefore to keep the organization focused and prevent it from trying to be all things to all people. Many organizations lose this focus and wind up with multiple number-one priorities that constantly compete with each other.

Because there is so much disagreement over what these statements are for, the whole concept of developing a vision and mission is often met with eye-rolling and skepticism. Compounding the problem is that many vision and mission statements are so vague and global that they all tend to sound the same. (In fact, Dilbert cartoonist Scott Adams has a mission statement generator on his website. It provides the reader with a generic-sounding mission full of today's buzzwords and then gives the option of selecting "regenerate." When this button is clicked, all of the buzzwords rearrange, but the message stays basically the same.) A standard example of a generic vision goes something like this:

> "We will be the premier provider of value-added customer-focused solutions in strategically chosen markets."

Sounds great, but what does it *mean*? It really doesn't shed any light on what the organization is about, what it is trying to achieve, or what will happen if it is successful. A CEO of a large health plan unveiled a new vision statement that claimed the organization would become "the premier health plan" in the area. When questioned about what the "premier" health plan meant, he commented that premier had to do with membership numbers, and that their plan membership would grow from 8 million to 15 million members within the next 5 years. Upon hearing this statement, half of the senior management team nearly passed out. It was *their* belief that "premier" meant a focus on refining and expanding the product line and the way service was delivered, but that growth may only increase from 8 million to 8.2 million or so in the process. Bottom line: It was clear that the management team that crafted the vision statement in this instance had completely different interpretations of its meaning, and the implications of this disagreement would be dramatic. It would obviously require a very different set of initiatives to move an organization from 8 million members to 15 million members versus the activities needed to firm up the product offering and move to 8.2 million members.

This is unfortunately not an isolated occurrence. Asking each member of an executive team individually about his or her vision of what the future will or should look like for the organization can be very instructive. Even a question as basic as, "What do you think our company's overall sales volume should be *next year*?" can be met with huge differences in interpretation. One insurance company executive team was questioned on the subject of projected premium to be written in the upcoming year, and they gave answers ranging from $75 million to $425 million. Some members of the senior team were hesitant to even give a number for fear of being embarrassed by their lack of knowledge. It would obviously be difficult for this company to mount any cohesive effort to achieve its goals.

How does an organization get in a situation where the leaders don't understand their vision? Admittedly, it sounds too fantastic to be true. But many organizations fall into the trap of planning in isolation; each functional part of the organization plans for its own department without regard to the whole. In these cases it is common for a human resources (HR) executive, for example, to know a great deal about HR and what the *department* is trying to accomplish, but be disconnected from what the *business* is trying to accomplish. Would the executive team members in charge of the support functions (e.g., HR, information technology (IT), finance) in *your* organization know the projections for the future and how they were determined? Would they understand the needs of your external customers? Many times the leaders of the support functions are unable to answer these questions. In fact, on occasion the managers even become hostile when asked about these issues, stating that "external customer needs have nothing to do with me because all my customers are *internal*." This view leads to the mentality that they have a separate mission and vision: to be a top-flight HR department or IT department or whatever. The harm in this is that a world-class IT department, for example, may have all the latest techno-toys and wonderful expertise, but this capability doesn't get properly translated to and utilized by the business. In other words, technology isn't leveraged, doesn't become a driver of organizational success, and operates in an isolated fashion. Thus the IT department comes to be viewed as a group that is distant, not focused on its internal customers, difficult to understand, not appreciative of the realities of the business, and so on; the list of common pitfalls is long.

The moral of the story is that the vision and mission shouldn't be global statements that don't do anything but satisfy the requirement that an organization should have a vision and mission. A good vision statement is a starting point to help the organization articulate "what it wants to be when it grows up." In other words, if the organization typically utilizes a five-year planning horizon when developing a strategy, the vision and mission should form a framework for the company to describe in broad terms what it will look like five years hence if it is successful.

After starting with the global statement, it is critical to nail down the specific parameters of what success looks like. The leadership development organization / fraternity Alpha Phi Omega is a good example of how a global vision can be translated into precise and measurable characteristics. Their mission statement is a rather all-encompassing *"To be recognized as the premier service-based leadership development organization."* But viewing their goals gives a much more precise description of what this actually means to them. It means (among other things) a membership retention rate of over 90%, 386 active chapters with 18,000 members, over 2,000 donors contributing a total of at least $175,000, a 25% increase in the volunteer base, the addition of five new international chapters, and more. The great thing about the list of goals is that it provides evidence that the organizational leadership has a clear view of what it wants the "premier" organization to look like in the future.

Microsoft had a vision statement many years ago that claimed that if it was successful, there would be "*a computer on every desktop.*" It was a great vision because it was short, easy to remember, and articulated precisely where they wanted to go. They modified their vision in recent years to incorporate the trends toward access and mobility versus being chained to the desktop, but retained the principles of keeping the vision short, precise, and easy to understand. The company also has a mission statement that states the reason it is in business is to "help people and businesses throughout the world realize their full potential." This certainly can aid in resource allocation decisions; the opportunities that will better enable them to achieve this mission would get priority.

Implementation: Creating the Statements

The execution of the strategic process depends on getting a good start; the view of the future must be understood and agreed on by the senior team before moving on to the next step. Developing the actual vision statement is an inexact science, but the following tips should make the process easier:

- *The five common elements to consider when developing a vision are finance, customer, process, technology, and people.* The purpose for considering these issues is to frame your view of what the ideal future would look like. It may help to structure discussion among the leadership team around some or all of the following questions: How would you define success financially? Who are your key customers, who should they be, and how are their needs changing? Why do they buy from you? What processes differentiate you from your competition (both positively and negatively)? What advances in technology will impact your industry in the future, and are you well-positioned to take advantage of them? What about your workforce gives you a competitive edge or disadvantage?
- *The conversation about these elements shouldn't be an all-day meeting.* Discuss each item for a reasonably short period of time to

ensure the entire team has the same general view of what the key issues are. Then select one person in the group to write a trial vision statement in two minutes or less. Don't try to write the perfect statement the first time. Groups often obsess about getting it exactly right, resulting in long-winded debates over each word or phrase. Instead, after a bit of discussion about key points, have somebody write *something*. It is generally much easier to critique and modify an existing statement than to create the perfect version from scratch. The group should rework and modify the statement until they all feel comfortable with it.

- *Sleep on it.* It is common for a statement to sound great at the end of a long meeting, but after rest and reflection the statement could prompt a reaction of "what were we thinking?" A review a day or two after the development session is advised.
- *Get feedback on the modified statement from stakeholders who were not part of the development process.* This can be midlevel managers, nonmanagement employees, trusted customers, suppliers, and so on. It is important to see if the message the leaders are trying to send is being picked up by those who were not a part of the discussion.

While it is great and important to have the actual statement, the more critical issue is to understand the parameters the organization is shooting for to define successful achievement. As previously stated, the vision typically will be global in nature and open to multiple interpretations. A useful technique to make it more tangible is as follows:

- Write the ending year of the planning horizon on a flipchart. (e.g., if the year is 2007 and the company is thinking through a five-year strategic plan, then write 2012 on the flipchart).
- Keep the vision in plain view and ask the question, "If we are successful in reaching this vision by the designated year, what will the organization look like when we get there?" In other words, describe the main characteristics of the organization if you drive it the way you are trying to drive it. Common topics include the total sales

dollars, number of customers projected, geographic spread of locations and customers, large internal process deployments, number of employees projected, and the like. (*Note:* Public sector and other not for-profit organizations should follow the same process steps. It may be necessary to modify the question of total sales dollars to be budget focused, but many of the rest of the questions will remain the same.) It is *very* important to keep this discussion high-level; the objective is not to split hairs and get everything correct to the third decimal place. Rather, the objective is to make sure there is broad agreement on the parameters. For example, suppose an organization currently does $100 million in sales with 500 employees. Some of the executive team members may project sales five years out to be $140 million. If others feel that $137 million is the proper number, you are close enough: pick one figure and move on. However, if some members feel this will be accomplished by growing the workforce to 750 employees while others feel the workforce must remain at 500, then *that* is a difference worth some discussion.

- This step should also not be an all-day discussion, and the resulting list of parameters should not be viewed as exhaustive or unchangeable. As long as the leadership team feels it has a consistent broad-stroke view of where it wishes the organization to go, then discussions have been successful. Record the final list of parameters to provide the framework for the rest of the process and move on.

Generally speaking, the development of a mission statement is not as involved or difficult as the vision, because it is usually much easier to answer "why are we here?" as opposed to "where are we going?" The principles of writing something down quickly and then critiquing it apply to missions as well as visions, and the rest is straightforward.

STRATEGIC ASSESSMENT

The strategic assessment step is designed to identify the critical issues that will impact your ability to get from your current state to the state outlined in the vision and mission. The assessment can be done in a variety of ways, ranging from the use of simple brainstorming to utilizing a variety of complex analytical tools.

Whatever methods are employed, the output of this step should be a list of strengths, weaknesses, opportunities, and threats (hereafter referred to as S.W.O.T.s). *Strengths* are those internal things that the organization is proficient in; they will better enable the organization to achieve the vision. Conversely, *weaknesses* are internal issues that will prevent the organization from achieving the mission and vision. *Opportunities* can be viewed in multiple ways. They typically involve "doing something the organization is not currently doing" that will help move it toward achieving the vision. This can be anything from acquiring a new business to providing management training to developing new products. This is a critical part of the assessment because it gives the leadership team the chance to be creative. Finally, *threats* are those things beyond the control of the organization that could negatively impact its ability to achieve the vision. Threats are typically viewed as external things such as potential new governmental legislation, economic downturn, weather-related catastrophes, and so on. But keep in mind that if a plan is being developed for a business unit within a larger organization, it is important to also consider threats such as hiring or budget freezes imposed by corporate, imposed pay scales that practically guarantee turnover, and the like. These issues are not external to the organization, but they are external to the business unit and can definitely make achievement of the plan more difficult.

Most strategic planning processes involve the identification of S.W.O.T.s, but for whatever reason these valuable pieces of information aren't fully utilized. It is common to develop a list of key issues and stick them in an appendix to the plan without really doing anything with them, but S.W.O.T.s are invaluable to the remainder of the process. They are used for the development of the strategic objectives, the identification and prioritization of strategic measures, and the finalization of the strategic initiatives. Determination of key S.W.O.T.s can be done formally or informally. Both approaches are presented in the following sections.

Implementation: Informal Assessment

Informal assessment is often done in small organizations, business units within a larger organization, or companies engaging in the strategic process for the first time. Small organizations or business units typically have a leadership team that wears many hats and is close to both customers and rank-and-file employees. These organizations are not as likely to have the need for (or resources to fund) more formal approaches. Companies engaging in the process for the first time are typically attempting to learn about strategy in addition to developing a plan, so the informal approach fits nicely.

Informal assessment identifies S.W.O.T.s through a structured brainstorming session with the leadership team. A facilitator will break the session into the four S.W.O.T. components and ask for ideas for each. In other words, the first step is to conduct a brainstorming session for *strengths*. The vision and associated parameters should be posted in the room, and the session should begin with the question, "What internal things are we good at that will better enable us to achieve the vision elements described?" The leadership team members should begin calling out ideas, and the facilitator should appoint a few scribes to write down the strengths as they are suggested.

It is important to use the proper technique when transcribing S.W.O.T.s. It is recommended that each issue be written on a separate sticky note and that each note contain two components: the *fact* and the *implications* of the fact. For example, it is common to ask leaders to brainstorm strengths and to hear someone say:

"People"

It is not advisable to proceed without digging beneath the surface to determine what about the people is consider to be a strength and what this strength is expected to do for the organization. A good facilitator should ask, "What about your people makes this a strength?" A possible result could be, "Our sales force has lots of experience." While this is better than simply writing "people," it still doesn't adequately clarify the benefit to be derived. Asking "What do we expect to get from an experienced workforce?" may yield the following properly written S.W.O.T.:

> Depth of sales force experience gives us credibility in the market-place, making us more likely to win new accounts.

Note that this version contains both the fact (depth of experience) and the implications (makes us more likely to win new accounts). The assessment process, even when conducted informally, could easily yield more than 150 S.W.O.T.s. Imagine 150 to 200 statements on sticky notes without sufficient detail; the lack of clarity would make any type of further analysis extremely difficult. Experience has shown that confusion over issues later in the process is an almost certain result. So instead of settling for a list of strengths such as:

- "Product development"
- "Leadership"
- "Technology"

The facilitator should press for details until properly written issues such as the following are developed:

- "We develop products faster than competitors, creating a window of opportunity for sales"
- "Our leadership team is full of excellent communicators, leading to common understanding of our vision and increasing the probability we will achieve it."
- "Internet distribution capabilities have opened markets to us that are closed to our competition"

Generally speaking, the determination of strengths takes between 30 to 60 minutes and results in a list of 50 to 60 issues. From a technique perspective, it is important to do strengths first. This gets everyone in a positive frame of mind. If you begin with weaknesses, it can put people on the defensive and limit creativity later in the process. Also from a technique perspective, the facilitator shouldn't be anxious to move on to the next phase whenever there is a moment of silence. Think about the main components of strategy while brainstorming: financial, customer, process, people, and technology. If the facilitator notices that very few strengths are listed that are technology-oriented, for example, it is useful to question the group specifically on what the technology strengths might be.

When the time comes to transition to *weaknesses*, the facilitator should again reference the vision and resulting parameters and ask the question, "What internal things are we *not* good at that could *prevent* us from achieving our vision?" It is again critical to make sure each issue is listed in a consistent fact plus implications of the fact format. Sample weaknesses include the following:

- "Systems changes make it impossible to get accurate and reliable historical data, negatively impacting our decision-making ability."
- "Decentralized structure results in clients having multiple contact points within our organization, causing inconsistent communication of account status."
- "Poor communication between HR and operating areas results in hiring delays and candidates who are mismatched for the positions for which they are interviewing."

Once again, it is common to spend around 30 to 60 minutes on weakness generation, and the resulting list could easily be 60 items or more long. One cautionary tip for the facilitator: When it comes to weaknesses, the group sometimes has a tendency to want to either (1) debate whether an issue is really true, or (2) try to discuss and fix the problem on the spot. Either tendency can be counterproductive to the generation efforts and should be discouraged. In the former case, debating the veracity of an issue often happens because someone gets defensive. It is important that a facilitator defuse this tension by pointing out that the purpose of identifying weaknesses is not to fix blame, but rather to document all the issues in the system; it may have nothing to do with the people or manager involved. For example, consider the system change weakness noted previously. This shouldn't necessarily be seen as an indictment of the CIO. Business conditions, acquisitions, mergers, and a host of other things could have contributed to the need to change and modify systems in the past. So the CIO should not go on the defensive and feel the need to justify why changes have occurred. If differences of opinion persist on whether a certain issue is truly a weakness or not, simple data collection is an option that could resolve things.

Trying to fix all problems on the spot is another common tendency that can easily quadruple (or more) the amount of time an organization spends on weaknesses during the informal assessment phase. The facilitator must *constantly* reinforce that the purpose of this session is simply to document all of the issues, not to fix them. If the group follows the path of trying to fix everything as they go, two things will happen: (1) an inordinate amount of time will be wasted on the few issues that are identified, and (2) creativity in issue identification will be diverted to issue resolution, resulting in a far less comprehensive list of weaknesses. So the objective should be documentation, not resolution.

The *opportunities* portion of the brainstorming is usually the most interesting. Viewing the vision and parameters of success and asking, "What can we do to help us move toward our vision?" is a good first step. A common mistake is to limit your thinking to only those things that are easily doable, practical, realistic, and inexpensive. A good set of opportunities should include things that really push the boundaries. Just because an idea is placed on a list of opportunities does not mean that the organization is bound to do it immediately. If no out-of-the-box ideas are considered, it will typically be tough to reach the aggressive parameters necessitated by the vision.

The first round of opportunities usually includes many items that could easily be replicated by your competitors (e.g., giving customers baseball tickets or taking them out for dinner). These are fine, but the leadership team should be encouraged to think about things that the competition will have a more difficult time duplicating. One useful technique for identifying these types of solutions is to think about the problems your customers face on a daily basis. (*Note:* These don't necessarily need to be problems with *you* or your organization; you should just think about the problems faced in general.) If the facilitator lists these problems and then questions the group on potential ways to solve some of them, it can frame a very interesting and powerful discussion. Some solutions and opportunities identified are typically things that are relatively easy to implement and yet are viewed as having great value by the customer. These opportunities help differentiate you from the competition and create strong long-term customer relationships.

A public-sector example might be useful to illustrate this point. Many years ago in most states, the process for renewing a driver's license was simple: Go to the Department of Motor Vehicles (DMV), wait in a line that was three city blocks long, get to the front, find out you are missing a single piece of necessary documentation, and as a result enjoy repeating the process a second time. In many states the DMV has realized that a problem its customers (i.e., the general public) face is that they are pressed for time. Spending a day on license renewal was not viewed as productive or enjoyable, and inevitable complaints about poor service were a certain result. An opportunity that may arise in a brainstorming session for a DMV leadership team may therefore be:

> Make alternate methods of license renewal available to enable customers to get their new license in a more convenient fashion.

This opportunity would solve the customer problem of lengthy renewals, reduce the complaints coming into the DMV, and perhaps even require fewer DMV personnel, depending on the registration options under consideration for implementation. Note the fact plus implications of the fact format applies to opportunities as well. Other examples of well-written opportunities are as follows:

- "Partner with a travel agency to provide access to travel information online to reduce employee frustration and save money."
- "Develop distributive print capabilities to enable us to improve customer convenience and print at their site."
- "Provide staff training in how to communicate with customers, which would help identify cross-selling opportunities and build long-term relationships."

The final segment of the brainstorming session should be dedicated to *threats*. The facilitator can open this discussion by once again referring to the vision and parameters of success and asking, "What external issues beyond our control could negatively impact our ability to achieve the vision?" The threats should be written in a format consistent with the rest of the S.W.O.T. categories. As noted earlier, *external* can be viewed as outside the entire organization for a company-wide strategic plan or external to the business unit for a lower-level strategic plan. Examples of well-written threats include:

- "Economic downturn would lead to decrease in recreational spending, impacting sales of almost all of our products."
- "Increasingly stringent regulations are forcing up our compliance costs and will soon result in either dramatic price increases or selling at a loss."
- "Hiring freeze imposed by corporate results in overloading our superstars and will eventually lead to turnover."

The threats portion of the brainstorming session tends not to last as long as the others, because many of the issues that are identified have already been discussed in some detail through the other categories. Thirty minutes is usually plenty of time to complete the brainstorming with a representative list of threats.

The entire process for S.W.O.T. generation described usually takes a half-day or less. Is it dangerous to build a strategy for the future based on a half-day of brainstorming opinions? It *could* be, dependent on several factors. Remember that this informal approach was recommended only in certain situations. For example, small organizations usually have a leadership team that wears many hats. The same executive may be responsible for various operational responsibilities as well as dealing with sales, hiring, and so on. The risk is minimized in this circumstance because the leaders are intimately familiar with most of the strategic building blocks. In other words, there isn't as much risk of missing critical process, people, and other factors that the executives wouldn't be familiar with. The same logic could apply to a business unit within a larger organization.

Another requirement for using the informal approach is a strong and cohesive leadership team. A strong team understands not only its own area of expertise but also how the interactions work among the different functions within the company. The requirement for a cohesive team is critical to make the S.W.O.T. generation session productive, versus an extended exercise in finger-pointing and denial.

Some tips and cautions will help make this process easier for the facilitator. First and foremost, it is inevitable that some of the issues surfaced during brainstorming will more naturally fit into other S.W.O.T. categories. For example, suppose the group is trying to identify weaknesses. One leader offers the following:

> Pay scale dictated from corporate is low relative to other area companies, resulting in constant loss of key employees.

According to the definitions, this may be considered to be a threat versus a weakness because it is imposed from outside. There are two ways to handle this idea when it is surfaced: (1) explain it is really a threat and recommend it be surfaced again later, or (2) transcribe it and add it to the list. The latter approach is strongly recommended. Remember that the objective of all the data generation is to get a representative list of the issues a company faces when trying to achieve a vision. The objective is *not* simply to create a technically perfect set of S.W.O.T.s. Don't engage or let participants engage in long-winded debates over whether one particular issue is a weakness or a threat.

Another tip is to create a matrix to tabulate the types of issues being raised. The columns of the matrix should be the S.W.O.T. categories, and the rows should be the five components of strategy (i.e., finance, customer, process, people, and technology) as shown in Exhibit 3.2.

As the ideas are called out in the brainstorming session, the facilitator (or someone appointed by the facilitator) should keep track of the types of ideas being suggested. For example, one of the leaders may suggest:

> Market services throughout Canada to attract new business.

This would be classified as a customer opportunity, so a check should be placed in the corresponding box on the matrix. Keeping track of

EXHIBIT 3.2   *S.W.O.T. Matrix*

	Strengths	*Weaknesses*	*Opportunities*	*Threats*
Finance				
Customer				
Process				
Technology				
People				

issues in this manner is a good way to minimize the probability that entire categories of issues are overlooked. The facilitator may direct questions to specific portions of the matrix to fill in gaps. In other words, "what technology weaknesses will prevent us from achieving our vision?" and so forth. Again, this will help minimize the probability that the informal assessment approach will result in missing key issues.

The output of this assessment will be a list of issues that will influence the organization's ability to achieve its vision, including internal and external positives and negatives. This list of issues will be utilized in developing the *strategy map*, to be discussed in later sections. If the organization is sufficiently large or complex and feels that the informal approach will not suffice, techniques for a more formal assessment are presented in the next section.

Implementation: Formal Assessment

Most organizations take a more formal approach to strategic assessment to ensure they have considered all vision-critical issues. The format of the formal assessment will vary from company to company, but many of the common questions are listed in Exhibit 3.3.

The questions on the left should be viewed as a menu, just like in a restaurant. When conducting an assessment, these are menu items to

EXHIBIT 3.3 *Formal Assessment Template*

Key Questions	Potentially useful tools
Financial perspective	
• What are the key financial indicators?	• Brainstorming
• What are the trends for the key indicators?	• Run/control charts
• What external factors will impact our financials?	• Brainstorming
• What is the budget for strategic plan execution?	• Sledgehammer
Customer perspective	
• What are the key customer segments?	• Brainstorming
• What are the key S.W.O.T.s surrounding relationships with key customer segments?	• System maps
• What "must-be's" of the relationships are not met?	• Kano analysis
• What can we do to "delight" each segment?	• Kano analysis
• What are our key competitors' strengths and weaknesses?	• Focus groups/ research
• How will the industry change in the future?	• Focus groups/ research
Process perspective	
• What are the S.W.O.T.s surrounding key internal relationships? (Including support functions)	• System maps
• Which processes have strategic significance in terms of gaps that need to be closed?	• Process maps
• Which processes have strategic significance in terms of strengths and capabilities to be leveraged?	• Process proficiency matrix
• What are the strengths and weaknesses of our product offering?	• Product worksheet
Learning & growth perspective	
• What does management think key S.W.O.T.s are?	• Mgmt interviews
• Does management have a consistent vision?	• Mgmt interviews
• How high is morale, and what are the key influences?	• Mgmt interviews/ employee focus groups
• Do employees understand the vision?	• Ee focus group/survey
• Do employees agree with management on 1 and 3?	• Ee focus groups/survey
• What future technology changes will impact us?	• Focus groups/research
• How will needed workforce skills change in the future, and are we prepared to be successful in that environment?	• Focus groups/research

select from. This doesn't mean that *every* question needs to be asked in *every* assessment. Also, most restaurants prepare dishes for customers upon request that are not listed on the regular menu. In the same way, these questions should not be viewed as exhaustive. It is common when doing an assessment that new and different questions will arise as you progress through the different categories.

In the right-hand column are tools and techniques that are commonly used to help answer the related question. The reader should note that it isn't *mandatory* to use the tools to answer questions; the tools are simply there to help when needed. It should be noted that, just like in the informal assessment, the goal of all the questions and tools is to establish S.W.O.T.s. The output of this assessment will look just like the output of the informal assessment, but this group of issues should be more comprehensive and voluminous. Because the main theme of this book is the linkage of process and strategy, the process assessment will be presented first and in the most depth. Financial, customer, and learning and growth assessment techniques will follow.

PROCESS ASSESSMENT: IMPLEMENTATION

For, the process assessment is typically the most difficult to execute successfully many reasons. The first is that a typical organization has thousands upon thousands of processes. When conducting an assessment, it is impossible to analyze all of them thoroughly to determine the S.W.O.Ts of each. Another complicating factor is that many organizations are so functionally focused that few people understand the flows of the major cross-functional processes. In other words, they understand their own *portion* of the process, but there's an overall lack of understanding of the *entire* process. This could limit the effectiveness of brainstorming key process S.W.O.T.s, because most issues identified through brainstorming will be of a functional versus cross-functional nature.

This tendency toward functional focus highlights a larger problem. The management team of an organization often doesn't have a thorough knowledge of its company's processes. This is obvious (and under-standable) when a manager is new to the organization, but it is also likely to be a problem when a manager has achieved a senior position through consistent promotions within the same functional area. It can be a serious barrier to both assessment and ongoing decision making if the management team doesn't have sound process understanding.

Another barrier to process assessment is that when most people think about processes in their organization, they inevitably think only about the negatives. If you ask the question, "What is the first thing that comes to mind when you think about the processes in your organization?" most people respond "They are bureaucratic," "They need to be streamlined," "They need serious upgrading," and so on. Very rarely is someone's first reaction "We have a great product development process" or something of that nature. The implication of this tendency is that an organization has to be careful that its assessment doesn't get overloaded with weak-nesses while neglecting strengths and opportunities.

Fortunately, all of these potential barriers are navigable through the formal assessment process. The first issue is the inability to thoroughly analyze thousands of processes because of time and resource con-straints. The good news is that it isn't necessary to do so. The point of the assessment is not to analyze everything; rather, it is to determine which processes have *strategic* significance. Two categories of processes may impact strategy: (1) those that seriously block the organization from meeting strategic goals, and (2) those that the organization does so well that leveraging their capability could take the organization to the next level. This is why the first two questions on the assessment tem-plate in the process section are as follows:

1. Which processes have strategic significance in terms of gaps that need to be closed?
2. Which processes have strategic significance in terms of strengths and capabilities to be leveraged?

The first question can be answered by using two tools common to process analysis: the *system map* and the *process map*. System maps are ideal tools for a strategic assessment because they evaluate *interactions*. It has been said that the job of a manager is not to manage *actions*, but to manage *interactions*. Managing actions is micromanagement. For example, it shouldn't be the role of the accounting manager to look over the shoulder of the accounts payable clerk to ensure that the steps of the accounts payable process are being followed, day in and day out. The job of the accounting manager should be coordination and integration of all the functions within accounting, such as accounts payable, accounts receivable, payroll, and so on. Then, as the accounting manager moves up to CFO and COO and CEO, the responsibility continues to be coordination and integration of more diverse areas. This means that by the time a manager reaches the level where he or she is devising strategy, he or she will need to have a familiarity with the large, cross-functional processes of the organization. Evaluating these interactions to determine S.W.O.T.s is ideally suited to the system map.

To understand the system map, it is instructive to begin with the basic components of the process, as illustrated in Exhibit 3.4.

Anyone familiar with process analysis and improvement is probably familiar with this basic chain of components. Starting in the middle, there is a box labeled P/D/C/I, which stands for Process-Department-Company-Industry. The system map is a flexible tool that can be used to evaluate the interactions of any of these units with its suppliers and

EXHIBIT 3.4 *System Model: Basic Components*

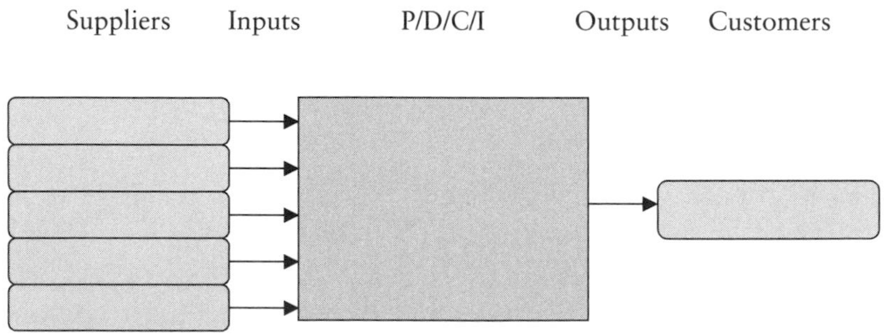

Suppliers	Inputs	P/D/C/I	Outputs	Customers

customers. *Processes* have customers that may be internal or external. For example, the cargo shipping process for an airline would have the receiver of the freight as a customer. The admissions process for a hospital would have a combination of external (the patient) and internal (doctors, nurses) customers. *Departments* have customers that are often other departments. This is easily seen when you consider the support functions of an organization. Human resources or information technology, for example, have internal customers consisting by and large of the rest of the organization.

Companies obviously have the external customer group consisting of the buyers of their product(s) or service(s), but they can also view their board of directors and shareholders as customers (from a private-sector perspective) and the legislature, taxpayers, and so forth as customers (from a public-sector perspective). *Industries* may share the same external customer groups as the company example, although evaluation would take a broader view. (Instead of looking at what Ford customers are looking for, for example, the objective would be to determine what *all* auto buyers are looking for.) So the first step in building a system map is to determine what frame of reference you want to use (i.e., select a process, department, company, or industry that has a customer or supplier relationship you want to analyze).

Whatever you choose for the box in the middle, it will have certain **inputs**, which are the key things that must be present for the P/D/C/I to get started. For the hospital admissions process, for example, the inputs could consist of a patient, a referral from an external physician, admission forms, and so on. For an HR department, inputs may be a job applicant, request for filling an open position from the hiring department, and the like. The inputs typically come from **suppliers**, which could be internal or external. In the previous examples, a patient or job applicant would obviously be external, while the requests and forms would come from internal sources.

Located to the right of the P/D/C/I box are the **outputs**, which are defined as what is produced from the P/D/C/I. For example, the output of the shipping process would be freight arriving at its desired location.

The output of a hospital would be a discharged and (hopefully) healthy patient. The output of an IT department would be (hopefully) smoothly running systems and projects completed on time and within budget. These outputs go on to the **customer**, which again could be internal or external.

Again, these components are not revolutionary concepts. Basic process mapping texts have discussed and explained these basic components for years. What differentiates the system map from basic process mapping tools is the remainder of the components, which focus on the *interactions* between the basic components. It begins with the fact that customers all have certain needs, which are referred to as *specifications and expectations*, or *specs and expects,* in Exhibit 3.5.

Specs are the formal needs of the customer being analyzed. Imagine drawing up a contract between your organization and the customer in question. Specs would be the items you would expect to be part of the contract. For example, how much would the product or service cost, when it would be delivered, how long it would be guaranteed to last, and so on. **Expects** are the informal needs of a customer. These things would never show up on a contract, but nevertheless are important to a customer. For example, customers want to know that your organization cares about them, has sympathy when there is a problem, is polite and helpful on the

EXHIBIT 3.5   *System Model: Customer Needs*

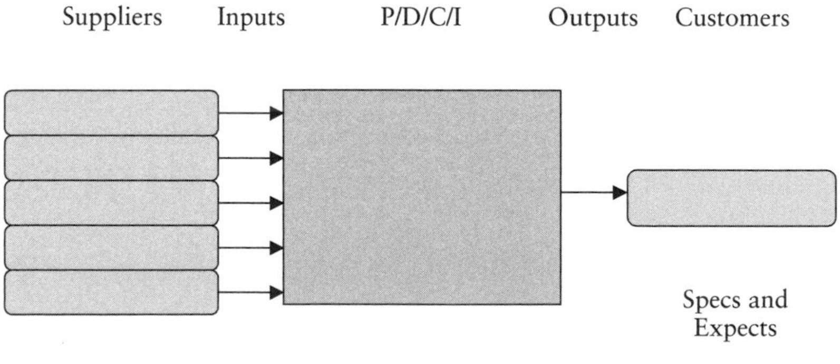

| Suppliers | Inputs | P/D/C/I | Outputs | Customers |

phone, and so forth. These things are critical to customer satisfaction, but typically wouldn't be part of a formal list of specifications.

The point is that to truly satisfy the customer of the P/D/C/I, the outputs must meet their formal and informal needs. Whenever the specs and expects are not met, there will be **gaps**, shown in Exhibit 3.6.

Gaps typically show up in terms of output and can come in any form: cost, service, speed, timeliness, friendliness, honesty, and the like. How does the organization know when it has gaps? Because customers will let you know. They provide feedback to your organization on both specs and expects to let you know how you are doing, much in the same way you provide feedback to your suppliers. These **feedback loops** are shown in Exhibit 3.7.

Feedback can be formal or informal. Formal feedback is typically initiated by the organization versus the customer. It is a concerted effort to proactively find out what the customers are thinking and how they feel. Examples of formal feedback would include surveys, phone interviews, and so on. Informal feedback is that which the organization is reliant upon customers to provide. This comes in the form of customer-initiated phone calls, e-mails, face-to-face discussion, and so on.

EXHIBIT 3.6 *System Model: Gaps in Meeting Customer Needs*

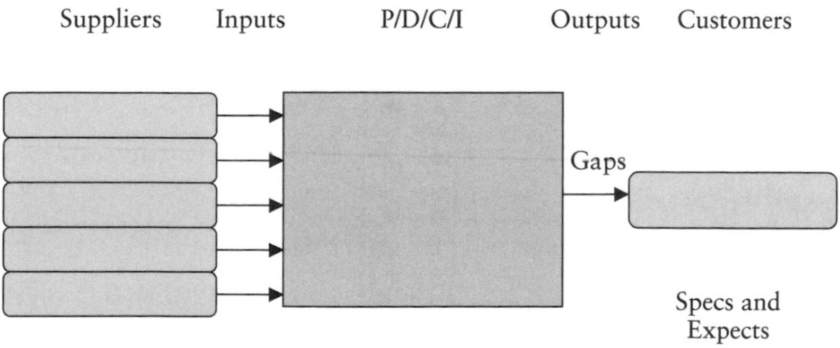

EXHIBIT 3.7   *System Model: Feedback Loops*

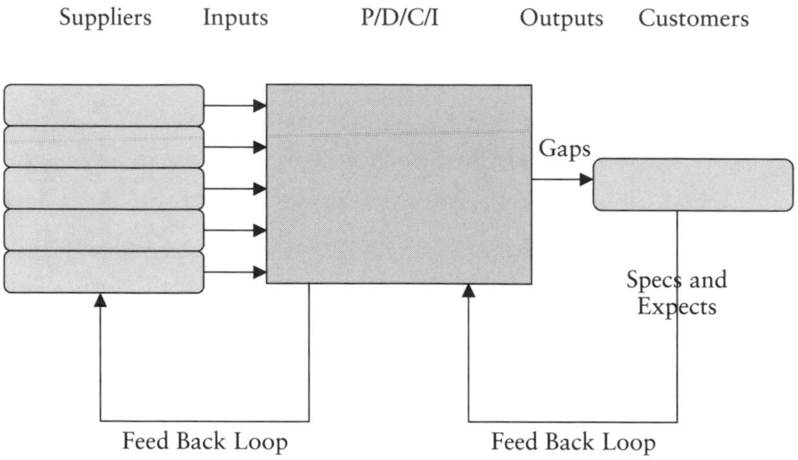

It is not advisable to rely solely on informal feedback to keep in touch with your customer base. This will put you in a prime position for over-reaction to a tiny subset of customers who have had either an extremely good or extremely bad experience with your organization. For example, think about the situation in which you would provide feedback to an airline regarding a flight you've recently taken. Very rarely would a passenger call an airline and say, "We took off from Houston about ten minutes late, made up most of the time in the air, and got in to Denver pretty much on schedule. The food was mediocre, and it took about ten minutes to get my bag—just wanted you to know." This type of flight experience would never prompt someone to sit down and provide feedback to the airline, and this is the experience most customers will have. What a passenger chooses to provide feedback on is the instance in which it took 24 hours to get from Houston to Denver, the gate agents were surly and uninformative, the plane was dirty and smelly, and their bags went to London. Or, on the other hand, when they were in a hurry and left their computer in the gate area and the airline tracked them down and returned it right before their big presentation. These extreme conditions are what prompt passengers to provide feedback on their own. While it is important to understand both the wonderful and terrible experiences passengers have had, it is dangerous to make management decisions based solely on the extremes. So, if no formal feedback mechanism is in place, it should be questioned whether a new one should be developed.

The term *feedback* is common and well-understood. The next component of the system map is typically less familiar, and deals with the communication going in the other direction. This type of communication is known as *feed forward*, and the **feed forward loops** are shown in Exhibit 3.8.

Feed forward is the way in which you help customers manage their expectations; it is how you let them know what to expect from you. For example, if you go to Disney World and want to get in line for one of the rides, there will always be a sign there telling you how long the wait will be. If the sign says 45 minutes, then a typical customer accepts that 45 is a minimum, and at other places this may be true. However, at

EXHIBIT 3.8 *Feed Forward Loops*

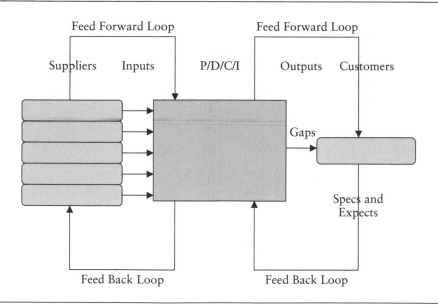

Disney World, 45 minutes will be the *maximum*. They have done studies that show that 45 would be a worst-case scenario; a sign saying 45 minutes usually means you will get on in 30 or 35. So if a customer gets in line thinking the wait is going to be 45 minutes long and winds up having to wait only 30, how would they feel? Probably quite good, happy, excited, and satisfied, because Disney set their expectations and then exceeded them.

This is the essence of what good feed forward is supposed to do: Let the customers know what is coming so they can be prepared. Think about the implications of not having good feed forward. If you don't help customers set their expectations, they have no choice but to set their own. The danger in this is that they could set their expectations so high that, even if you do everything perfectly, you could wind up disappointing them. Imagine the Disney waiting-in-line scenario in the absence of a sign. If customers got in line for one of the rides and expected to wait 10 minutes, how would they feel when the actual wait time was 30 minutes? In all likelihood they would feel angry and upset, and this impression would stick with them for the rest of the day. The instructive point here is that the same 30-minute wait would be perceived completely differently by the customer, depending on whether good feed forward was present or not.

These are the components of the system map. As has been noted, it can be an extremely valuable tool for evaluating key relationships during the strategic assessment phase of the process. There are two common applications: (1) how a company interacts with its external customers, and (2) how key internal departments serve as customer and supplier to each other. The former application is best suited for the customer portion of the assessment, and the latter application is ideal for the process portion of the assessment. Because the first question in the process assessment section is, "What are the S.W.O.T.s surrounding key internal relationships?" the first system map example will be of an internal nature.

Not every organization will have the same internal relationships designated as *key*. An insurance company, for example, may consider the relationship between underwriting and claims to be critical. On the other hand, a company responsible for customizing its product offering to meet individual client needs may consider the relationship between sales and manufacturing to be vital to future success. While there will be industry-specific differences such as these, it is a given that relationships between key support functions (which could include HR, IT, Finance, Purchasing, etc.) and the core business should be analyzed via the system map. The purpose in analyzing these relationships is to determine whether the support functions truly provide support or are working for their own purposes. The following example will focus on HR, work through the development of the system map step-by-step, and describe the identification of S.W.O.T.s upon completion of the diagram.

A blank system map template is shown in Exhibit 3.9.

EXHIBIT 3.9   *System Map Template*

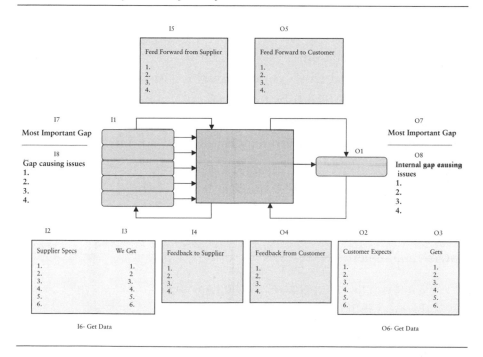

Note that the right-hand side of the map has positions labeled O1 through O8. This is typically referred to as the *output* side of the diagram, and it is necessary to answer a series of output questions to complete it. The left-hand side is referred to as the *input* side of the diagram, and there are eight additional questions (I1 through I8) to be answered to complete it as well. The designations O1 to O8 and I1 to I8 are listed on the template at the place in which the answer to the corresponding question should be written. The user will find that the learning curve for creating a system map is very steep. In other words, after you have done it once or twice, you probably will not need the questions anymore. However, they can be useful as a sort of cheat sheet while you become familiar with the tool. The relevant questions are listed as follows:

System Output Questions (O1–O8)

1. Who is your customer?
2. What are the customer's expectations of you? (Be as specific as possible.)
3. How do you think the customer would rate your level of service for each expectation?
4. How do you get feedback to know this customer is satisfied?
5. What forms of feed forward do you use to help set and manage customer expectations?
6. What gaps exist between expectation and output? Can these be quantified with data?
7. Which is the most important gap to your customer?
8. What internal processes and issues create this gap?

System Input Questions (I1–I8)

1. What suppliers contribute to the gaps in customer service? Select the most influential one(s).
2. What are your expectations of the key supplier(s)? (Be as specific as possible.)

3. What outputs does the supplier actually deliver to you? (How would you rate *their* service?)

4. How do you give the supplier(s) feedback to evaluate their performance?

5. What forms of feed forward do the supplier(s) use to help set and manage your expectations?

6. What gaps exist between your expectations and output? Can these be quantified with data?

7. Which is the most important gap to you?

8. What are the causes of this gap?

To complete an example analyzing the HR support function, the first step is to fill in the P/D/C/I box in the middle with HR. Then it is possible to begin answering the designated questions. Output question number one reads "Who is your customer?" There are many alternatives for how to answer this question, depending on what you need to know. For example, if this were a process improvement example and the objective was for an HR process team to determine how well the hiring process was working, the options for customer groups could be "hiring managers" or "applicants." If the objective were to determine compliance with hiring regulations, the customer might be "regulators." Because the purpose of this particular map is strategic assessment and the goal is to analyze the relationship between HR and other internal departments, the answer to this question can simply be listed as "Operations," as shown in Exhibit 3.10.

Questions two and three on the output side deal with customer expectations and how well they are being met. Question two reads, "What are the customer's expectations of you?" and there is an instruction to be as specific as possible. From a facilitation perspective, it is a good idea to have representatives from both HR and operations in the room to talk through the answers to these questions and complete the system map. A good technique at this point is to ask the HR representatives to give their opinion on what the operations people need from them. After they list several items, prompt the operations people for their opinions

EXHIBIT **3.10**   *Human Resources System Map*

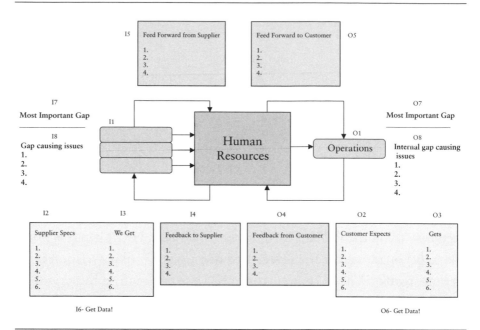

in order to determine how accurate and complete the list is. The supplier department (HR in this case) sometimes has a skewed view of what its customer truly needs. This may be grounds for a weakness to add to the S.W.O.T. list.

When question two has been answered, there will be an agreed-upon list of customer expectations. Question three reads, "How do you think the customer would rate your level of service for each expectation?" The question is phrased in this fashion to encourage the facilitator to use a similar approach to the one described in the prior question. Ask the HR representatives to predict how the operations people would rate HR's level of service for each requirement, using a scale of Excellent–Good– Fair–Poor. The purpose of this is twofold. First, it will help determine whether the two groups have a consistent view of the service being provided. Having HR present its view first is a good way to initiate this. Second, in most cases the supplier department is more critical of itself than the customer department is. This avoids the potential group dynamics roadblock of putting one department in the position of criticizing the other. At any rate, completing questions two and three and listing them on the map could yield something like Exhibit 3.11.

In this particular organization, there were two ratings of "poor." One deals with HR's inability to fill open positions, and the other deals with inconsistent application and administration of reward and recognition systems. While it is inadvisable to make a concrete rule that *every* "poor" identified through system mapping will beget a weakness for the list of S.W.O.T.s, it is a good practice to question whether the "poor" items have strategic significance. In this case inconsistent application of reward and recognition could possibly lead to turnover of key personnel, so this definitely could have strategic ramifications. Looking at the other extreme, note that there is a rating of "excellent" for providing adequate training. This could also have strategic significance. If the company is looking to expand its horizons by adding a new service line or will be adding a substantial number of employees for growth purposes, it is definitely significant that HR has the capability to sufficiently get them up to speed.

The next few questions deal with communication between HR and the operating areas. Question four asks how operations provides feedback to HR to let them know (1) what their needs are, and (2) how well HR is meeting them. The real issue here is whether any formal type of feedback exists. If there are no surveys or tools of that nature administered by HR, it is incumbent upon operations to continually communicate their needs. This could lead to a communication and coordination problem. Question five asks how HR provides feed forward to operations to help them manage their expectations. (In other words, how does HR let operations know what is going on in HR that will eventually impact them.) The results for these questions are shown in Exhibit 3.12.

The feedback is indeed primarily informal in this case. It is an open question whether lack of a formal survey is a gap large enough to prompt attention from the organization. The feed forward appears to be a combination of formal and informal. Benefit briefings are definitely a

EXHIBIT 3.11   *System Mapping Customer Expectations*

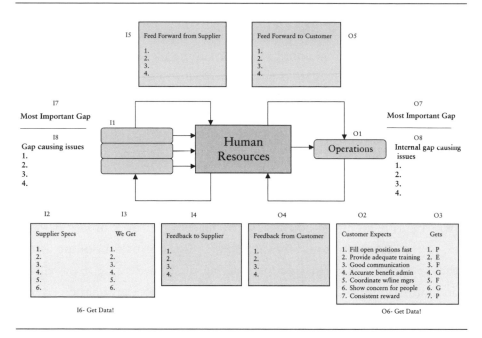

EXHIBIT 3.12   *System Mapping Customer Communication*

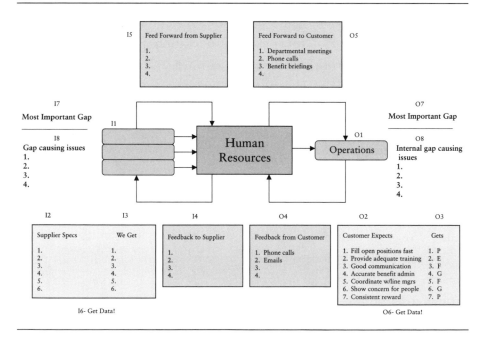

formal kind of feed forward, and departmental meetings may be as well. Obviously, the objective in both the feed forward and feedback boxes is to get quality versus quantity. The facilitator should look at the entire list of issues and ask whether the mechanisms listed are sufficient to keep supplier and customer on the same page.

Output question six reads, "What gaps exist between expectation and output?" The purpose of this question is to collect data whenever possible to either confirm or deny the perceptions presented and evaluated in the customer expectations box. For example, the first item operations deemed critical was to fill open positions quickly. Assume that an agreed-upon acceptable target for filling open positions might be 45 days. Operations gave HR a rating of "poor," suggesting that they believe that HR was quite ineffective in meeting the required timeline. There are two possibilities here: (1) either HR really *is* deficient in meeting the accepted time frame, in which case it may be necessary to analyze the process, or (2) HR does very well in meeting the 45-day target, but for whatever reason operations has the *perception* that there are problems. This could be due to many factors, but the point is that fixing the process is not the best course of action here—fixing the perception is. This could be worthy of inclusion on the S.W.O.T. list.

Questions seven and eight on the output side are designed to determine what are the causes of some of the bigger gaps in the relationship between customer and supplier. Question seven reads, "Which is the most important gap to your customer?" The group should look over the list of items in the customer expectations box in the lower right-hand corner of the diagram and identify which one is causing the most pain for the customer. In other words, which gap would the customer want closed more than any other. Once this has been selected, the group should think through what internal issues might be contributing to the gap. These will be listed under output question eight. Responses from this organization are listed in Exhibit 3.13.

Filling open positions in a timely fashion was the top-priority gap according to the group. The causes for this gap are listed in output question eight. Incomplete information from managers is the top gap-causing issue

EXHIBIT **3.13** *System Map Gap Prioritization*

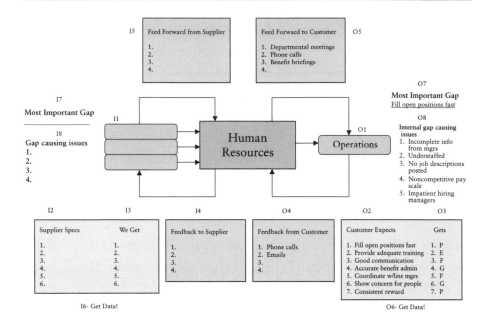

listed. This is a significant finding because the information needed to fill a position generally comes from the same operations people who are unhappy with poor service from HR. In other words, the operations people could be causing their own problem in this case. The same could be said for the issue regarding lack of job descriptions. These are supposed to come from the hiring manager, and not having one could result in HR improperly screening candidates. This could obviously send the entire process back to the drawing board. A noncompetitive pay scale could result in many rejections of job offers, lengthening the process as well. All of these issues may have strategic significance, depending on their severity.

A common mistake made by first-time facilitators is thinking they must select one issue *only* as the answer to, "what is your most important gap?" If there are two or three issues relatively even in importance, it is permissible (and advisable) to look for gap-causing issues for each one. In the HR example, it is quite possible that looking for gap-causing issues for inconsistent reward and recognition, for example, would yield another list of critical items for the S.W.O.T. list.

The output side of the map is now complete. The questions led the group through a discussion of customer needs and how well they are being met (both perceived and actual, if the relevant data was collected), the lines of communication open between customer and P/D/C/I, the number-one problem in the key customer's eyes, and a host of internal issues that contribute to the problem. This is already a considerable amount of potentially valuable information, but to complete the picture it is necessary to look at the input side as well.

The first question on the input side is, "What suppliers contribute to the gaps in customer service?" The purpose of this question is to select the entities external to HR that will provide products or services HR needs to satisfy the selected customer group. In the given example, suppliers may include the operating departments, corporate HR, regulators that set compliance policy, and so forth. These are illustrated in Exhibit 3.14.

It is a good practice to list the suppliers in order of the perceived impact on the ability to meet customer expectations. This hierarchy would imply that the organization felt like operations had the most impact on HR's ability to meet the needs of operations (which isn't unusual), followed by corporate HR and finally regulators.

Because operations has been selected as the supplier with the most impact, the next two questions on the input list are as follows:

- What are your expectations of the key supplier(s)?
- What outputs does the supplier actually deliver to you?

These questions should be answered with only operations in mind. In other words, what does HR expect or need from operations in order to provide good service to operations as a result? And how would HR rate the operations level of service (Excellent–Good–Fair–Poor) in each one of these categories.?

EXHIBIT 3.14   *System Map Suppliers*

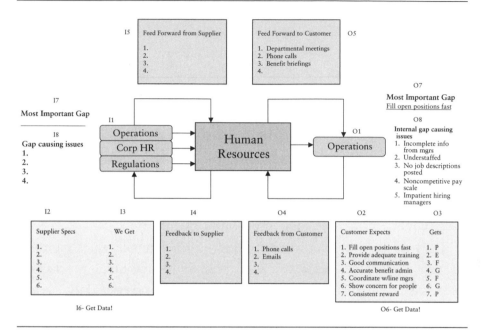

It is rare for one single supplier to be the determining factor in *all* gaps on the customer side. If corporate HR also is a significant contributor to gaps, then questions two and three should be answered again with a focus on corporate HR. The process should be repeated until all suppliers that have a significant impact on HR's ability to deliver good service have been discussed. In the example for this organization, it was felt that the top two suppliers (operations and corporate HR) have significant impact on the ability to deliver good service, but regulators did not. Therefore, the resulting system map is shown in Exhibit 3.15, with a dividing line between those requirements needed from operations and the ones aimed at corporate HR.

There are several significant findings in this portion of the map. First and foremost, operations is clearly contributing to its own problems. The failure to provide clear job requirements can directly impact the ability to fill open positions quickly, and the failure to provide adequate

EXHIBIT 3.15 *System Map Supplier Gap Analysis*

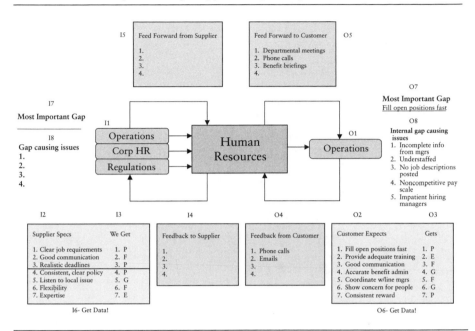

lead time with requests probably contributes to a perception gap that HR never gets things done on time. Both of these may be significant findings to add to the list of strategic S.W.O.T.s. With regard to the relationship to corporate HR, the fact that policy is not clear or consistent could certainly handcuff the ability of local HR departments to deliver quality service. Looking at the other extreme, the "excellent" rating for corporate expertise may lead to multiple strategic advantages.

Questions four and five on the input side revisit the communication links between suppliers and the P/D/C/I. The links between operations and HR were established on the output side, and many are simply reprinted on the map, and the links between HR and corporate HR have been added in Exhibit 3.16.

Nothing especially significant was revealed by the communication questions in this example, although perhaps the fact that corporate and

EXHIBIT 3.16 *System Map Supplier Communication Links*

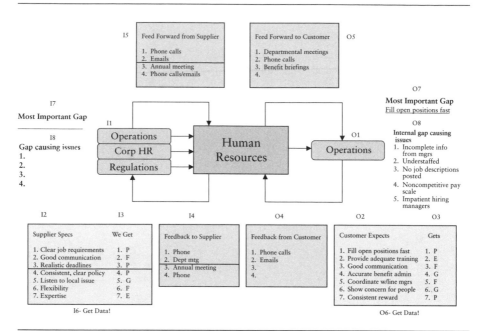

local HR meeting only once a year would be something to think about; more frequent meetings may be useful.

The next question (input question six) deals with the collection of data to confirm or deny the presence and severity of gaps on the supplier side. Just as it was on the output side, the intent here is to determine whether the gap is factual or perceptual. Things like policy changes can seem to happen all the time because they cause local people such a headache, but in reality it may not happen very often.

Question seven on the input side reads, "Which is the most important gap to you?" This is analogous to the same question on the output side, but this time HR gets to choose which of the input gaps *they* most want to see closed. The one selected by the HR department in the example is clear job requirements. This springs from the tendency of the hiring departments to not be specific enough when telling HR to find candidates to fill a certain position. As noted previously, this results in HR recruiting and interviewing people who are ill-suited to the position in question, causing delays in the ability to fill open positions.

The final question (input number eight) reads, "What are the causes of this gap?" The intent is to determine why, in this case, the hiring departments are not being clear in their requirements. Several potential causes for this phenomenon are listed in the now completed system map shown in Exhibit 3.17.

Typically it takes around an hour with a small group to complete a system map, with potential additional work needed for data collection. When complete, it is standard to think about what key learning points need to be added to the S.W.O.T. list. For example, the list of S.W.O.T.s could be as follows:

- "Hiring departments do not provide clear job requirements, resulting in delays in filling open positions and causing poor customer service."
- "Corporate HR is constantly changing policies and procedures, forcing local department to spend undue time on ensuring compliance versus serving internal customers."
- "Inconsistent application of the reward and recognition policy hurts morale and leads to turnover of key personnel."
- "Pay scale is not competitive with other companies in the area, which results in higher turnover"
- "Pay scale is not competitive with other companies in the area, which results in higher first offer refusal rate and delays hiring new personnel"
- "HR department cares about our people and their issues, which increase morale"

Note that all are written in the fact plus implications of the fact format, as always. It is common to get around a half-dozen key issues from each system map discussion. Having said this, keep in mind there shouldn't be a target number. The issues that will have an impact on the ability to achieve the vision are the ones that should be noted, whether there are two or twenty.

EXHIBIT **3.17** *Complete System Map*

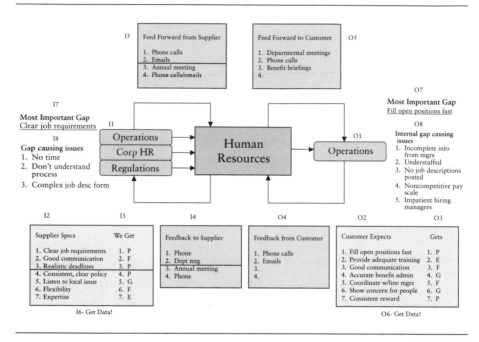

Recall that the purpose of the map is to assist in answering the first question from the process section of the strategic assessment template that reads, "What are the S.W.O.T.s surrounding key internal relationships?" System mapping sessions should almost always be set up to discuss the relationships between HR—Operations, IT—Operations, and Finance—Operations. These are support functions that every organization typically has and that need to be sufficiently plugged into the rest of the business to achieve any meaningful vision. After the three standard applications, it is up to the facilitator to determine which internal relationships are worthy of analyzing via system mapping sessions. It is not uncommon to spend a day or two conducting system mapping sessions to uncover the relevant internal S.W.O.T.s.

STRATEGIC PROCESS IMPROVEMENT

The second process assessment question from the template reads, "Which processes have strategic significance in terms of gaps that need to be closed?" In other words, which processes are prime candidates for *strategic improvement*. If you ask a typical employee what comes to mind when thinking about the processes in his or her organization, the first response will typically be negative. Common answers are things like "They are bureaucratic," "They need streamlining," "They don't work," "they take too long," and so forth. Very rarely do people think about the positive aspects of their processes first; the natural tendency is to think about how to fill the gaps. For this reason, *strategic process improvement* is the most common technique for illustrating how processes can drive strategy. The idea behind strategic process improvement is to determine which of the organization's processes are the most vital to future organizational success and ensuring that these processes are running at peak efficiency. And if they aren't, fixing them so they are!

The Chrysler product development case presented in Chapter 1 is an excellent example of a process that would need to be targeted for strategic improvement. Successful automakers *must* be able to predict consumer desires and develop and deliver the models that will satisfy them. It has been referenced that the idea-to-showroom-floor cycle time prior to the AMC acquisition was five years. Chrysler obviously identified product development as one area in need of strategic improvement. Following the acquisition, Chrysler looked at how AMC executed this process and noticed significant differences. At Chrysler, product development had been managed *functionally*. The process at AMC was more team-based. Groups of people from different departments brought diverse expertise to the table and worked together from the beginning. This enabled each area to have a say in the decision making and help them identify potential conflicts and resolve them on the spot. Chrysler modified its process to incorporate some of AMC's practices, and the results were dramatic. The idea-to-showroom-floor cycle time was reduced by over two years, and new products became the backbone of the Chrysler resurgence in the early 1990s. The Dodge Viper debuted in 1992, Chrysler Concorde in 1993, the redesigned Dodge Ram in 1994, the Chrysler Cirrus and Dodge Stratus in 1995—all giving the buying public something new and different to look at. The success continued with the introduction of the truly innovative PT Cruiser in 2001, which has been a strong selling model for the company ever since.

The merger that created DaimlerChrysler in 1998 intensified the focus on product development. In 2001 the company announced further process changes and improvements. The first was that the new product teams would be arranged by vehicle type versus specific model. Five classes (i.e., small vehicle, premium vehicle, family vehicle, activity vehicle, and truck) were named, giving the teams even more opportunity to share information and avoid the silo effects from the old days. A second change was the integration of purchasing specialists into the teams to make for more cost-effective buying for all vehicle lines. Further standardization across the company's main product lines (Chrysler, Mercedes, Mitsubishi) enabled the teams to further reduce costs by leveraging economies of scale while simultaneously reducing development time.

Another excellent example of strategic process improvement comes from Domino's Pizza. The chain began as a single store in Ypsilanti, Michigan, in 1960 and has grown into a multibillion-dollar juggernaut today. Their growth has been largely the result of process innovation. Domino's pioneered some of the changes in its industry that we know as commonplace today. A key process in the pizza delivery business has always been the ordering process. Domino's and its competitors obviously want to make this process as simple and painless for the consumer as possible. Many years ago, the more popular chains risked business loss because it simply took too long to process customer orders. It was common for a queue to back up on the phone, with customers being forced to wait to place orders and frequently giving up and ordering elsewhere.

Domino's started by creating a customer database with names, addresses, and ordering history. Whenever a customer called to place an order, the Domino's employee immediately had the information handy.

This eliminated the need to ask for and write down directions. It also sped up the process time to take an order, which reduced the time customers spent in the queue waiting for the store to pick up the phone. Because most competitors have benchmarked and adopted Domino's process, having a delivery chain ask for your phone number so they know who and where you are is now commonplace. It is easy to forget that not long ago this was a real customer headache.

So how does an organization identify the key processes during the assessment process? This is a challenging question to answer because of the aforementioned multitude of processes in most organizations. If an organization has 10,000 processes, then it is a fair bet that most people in the organization will feel that at least 9,999 of them could stand to be improved. So trying to settle on the vital few that will have the most significant strategic impact is quite a challenge. (The good news is that some of these processes may be identified in the prior system mapping exercise when evaluating key internal relationships. For example, a system mapping workshop evaluating the Sales–Manufacturing relationship may identify a key gap-causing issue as lack of communication, leading to an unsuccessful product development process.)

Fortunately, there are tools that help with the identification of processes targeted for strategic improvement. The tool listed in the template is the process map. Most people are at least somewhat familiar with basic flowcharting; documenting a step-by-step flow of how a process works. A process map, illustrated in Exhibit 3.18, adds the dimension of accountability to the standard listing of steps.

What differentiates a process map from a standard flowchart is the issue of accountability. Note that there are swim lanes drawn across the map. The people or departments that are involved in the process each have their own swim lane, and each step of the process is documented in the swim lane of the department responsible for execution of that step.

This particular example comes from IBM Credit and is an excellent example of the value of looking at processes cross-functionally. As noted in Chapter 1, many organizations are highly functionally focused. The standard approach to improvement of cross-functional processes in

EXHIBIT 3.18   *IBM Credit Process Map*

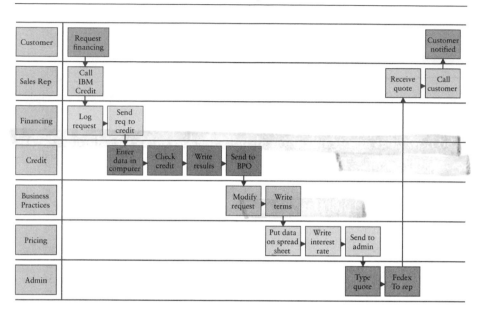

Adapted from Reengineering the Corporation

a functionally focused organization is to have each function try to improve its own individual piece of the process. This example illustrates
the fallacy of that approach.

IBM Credit is not in the business of making computers; it is in the
business of financing them. The process map illustrates the steps customers have to go through to gain approval for financing after they have
made the decision to buy an IBM computer. Note how many departments are involved and steps are necessary to tell a customer "yes, we'll
let you buy a computer from us." The cycle time to complete this process
was roughly *six days*. If you were a sales representative, what would your
perspective be on this? Almost certainly you would not be pleased, since
it gives the prospective customers a long time to think about their purchase and potentially change their mind. IBM Credit felt the same way,
so it set out to reduce the cycle time.

The traditional approach to process improvement at the time was to
have each department do its share to reduce its portion of the cycle time.

So in this case, the Financing department manager would work with his or her people to improve the steps of financing, the Business Practices manager would work with his or her people to improve the steps of business practices, and so forth. The thinking was that if each area improved its portion of the process, the cycle time would be dramatically reduced.

But IBM Credit approached it another way. If you have ever seen a relay race on television, you would probably agree that there are two ways for a team to lose a race. One way is simply to not run fast enough. To be sure, only one team runs fast enough to win. But if a team loses because it doesn't run fast enough, usually it only loses by a small margin. If a team loses a relay race by a *lot*, it typically is as a result of dropping the baton versus lack of speed. As IBM Credit looked at the process map, it realized that so many handoffs were built into the process that a lot of baton passing was going on. So they astutely questioned how much time was being spent actually working on the process versus passing the work back and forth. Studies revealed that out of the six days of *cycle* time, only about two hours of *process* time were being spent working on these requests. The rest of the time the requests were being handed from one person to the other or sitting in employees' in-boxes and out-boxes.

The traditional approach to process improvement clearly would not work here. If each manager worked with the employees in the individual departments to improve the processing time of their individual link, they might shave the processing time down from two hours to ninety minutes. While this would represent a 25% decrease in *process* time, the *cycle time* would still be six days! The problem lies in the handoffs, which are cross-functional issues. Traditional functional flowcharts will not bring this type of problem to light, which highlights the benefits of this type of process map.

The instructive point from a strategic perspective is that, as noted earlier, a good manager needs to manage *interactions* versus *actions*, and this type of chart highlights the interactions. This is one of the reasons why the process map is listed as a tool for the strategic assessment.

Another benefit of using the process map for assessment will be illustrated through the following example:

Bubble Production Process: Understanding Process Constraints

A critical concept for managers to be comfortable with is that of understanding process constraints. This will be illustrated by means of a simple example. The demo requires a bottle of bubble-blowing solution, two wands used to blow the bubbles, a ruler, and a flipchart with marker. Suppose five people are set up in line at the front of a room, and their job is to execute the bubble production process. Each person should be given a specific role, defined as follows:

- **Dipper:** responsible for placing a wand in the bottle of bubble solution, removing it, and placing it in front of the . . .
- **Blower:** responsible for positioning near the wand and blowing the bubbles into the air
- **Catcher:** responsible for taking the second wand, selecting a bubble while they are all in the air, catching the bubble on the wand, and presenting it to the . . .
- **Measurer:** responsible for taking a ruler and holding it next to the bubble, and calling out the size so the . . .
- **Recorder:** responsible for listening to the measurer; can write the number on a flipchart

The group should be given a five-minute time limit to begin producing bubbles. Anyone else in the room should observe as the process is executed so an accurate process map can be drawn at the end of the five-minute time period. The resulting process map is shown in Exhibit 3.19.

There are several instructive things about this process map. For example, note that both the dipper and the blower inspect for film. The dipper wants to make sure that the wand goes to the blower with ample solution in the wand, and the blower doesn't want to huff and puff to no avail if no bubbles are going to come out of the wand, so both have a compelling reason to check. But there is no question this is a redundant step, unnecessary to do twice.

EXHIBIT 3.19 *Bubble Production Process Map*

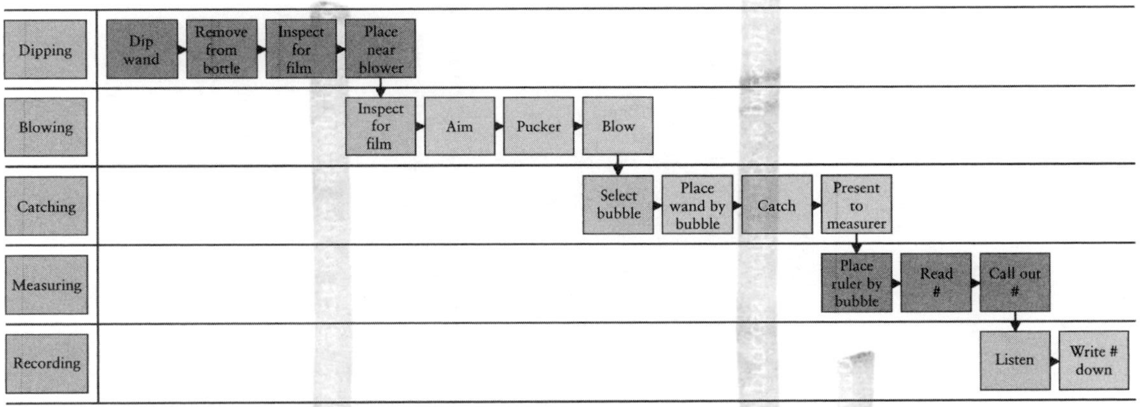

In the real world, this sort of thing happens all the time. Two departments do exactly the same thing because either (1) one department doesn't know the other is doing it, or (2) the second department (the "blower") got the equivalent of a wand with no solution in it from the first department (the "dipper") 17 years ago, so they have been checking for it ever since. Just as common and even more sad, sometimes the person who had the job before the person who had the job before the current dipper presented the person who had the job before the person who had the job before the current blower a wand with no solution in it 30 years ago, and everyone in both departments has now been checking for it ever since, even though nobody knows why anymore. This type of legacy process inefficiency is present in many organizations.

It follows that another big plus of the cross-functional process map is that it can identify repetitive efforts between departments. Note that a functional flowchart illustrating the steps in the blowing process alone would not have illustrated this redundancy, nor would a functional flowchart of the dipping process. Therefore, a leadership team must understand the big-picture cross-functional process flows within their organization; they are the only ones high enough in the organization to understand and identify areas of potential overlap.

Another important point from this demo is to note that there was no mention of objectives given to the group prior to the beginning of the process. This was intentional. In almost every case, the process operators will assume that the objective is to produce and record *big* bubbles. The blower and dipper go slowly to try and create big bubbles, but even then it is obvious that the catcher cannot catch them all. Out of every ten bubbles to come out of the wand, the catcher is lucky to catch one or two of them. Imagine how the process would change if, after a few minutes, the facilitator mentioned that in prior groups there has never been an instance where less than 20 bubbles were recorded on the flipchart. All of a sudden the dipper and blower would speed up because they are not worrying about bubble size, and it would become even more evident that the catcher could not keep up; bubbles would be hitting the floor all over the place.

This phenomenon has far-reaching implications. An important point is that even though the names of the departments in the process (and even the steps executed) would be identical whether the objectives were bubble volume or bubble size, the behavior of the process operators would be very different. This illustrates how important it is that everyone who has responsibilities for execution of a cross-functional process understands the *whole* process instead of just their portion of it. So the job of management is to manage the overall process, not to try to optimize each part of it. *This means that management cannot reinforce and reward functional behavior at the expense of process behavior.*

A more important point is the determination of which processes have strategic significance. Suppose the bubble example was revisited and you went department by department, trying to determine the capacity of each. For example, start with dipping and look at it in isolation. In other words, instead of considering the entire process, assume you are in the dipping business, and all you are responsible for is what is shown in Exhibit 3.20.

Think about the capacity of the dipping process. In other words, if the dipper never had to wait for the blower, how many bubbles could be blown from all the solution that could be dipped out of the bottle in, say, one minute? Assume that the latest in bubble-dipping data collection technology helped establish that the correct number was 150 bubbles per minute.

Now assume that the second company is in the bubble-*blowing* business. As such, all this organization is responsible for is the steps in Exhibit 3.21.

EXHIBIT 3.20 *Dipping Process*

EXHIBIT 3.21   *Bubble-Blowing Process*

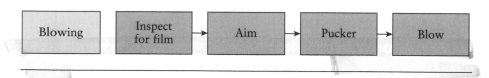

The assumption to be made this time is that the blower never has to wait on the dipper. In other words, the wand is always positioned, full of solution, and ready for the blower to begin. To understand capacity, the question that must be asked is how many bubbles could be blown in one minute (without hyperventilating!). Assume that the latest in bubble-blowing data collection technology helped establish that the correct number was 225 bubbles per minute.

The third company is in the catching business. The catching process is illustrated in Exhibit 3.22.

The assumption to make in this instance is that there are always bubbles in the air for the catcher to pick from, so there is never a need to wait for the dipper and blower. Further assume that there is no delay time waiting for the measurer on the back end; the bubble is measured instantaneously and the process is repeated. So how many bubbles could be caught and presented in one minute? It would realistically take about five seconds to do each one, so the capacity would be around twelve per minute.

The fourth company is in the measuring business, following the process shown in Exhibit 3.23.

The assumptions in this step are critical. Assume that the measurer *does not have to wait for the catcher.* Recall that the objective at the beginning of the exercise was to look at the capacity of each department *in isolation.* Therefore, the question is how many bubbles could be measured without the constraint of having to catch them first. So if there was always a bubble sitting on the wand waiting to be measured, it could probably be measured in less than two seconds, so the capacity for a minute would be around 45 bubbles.

The last company is in the recording business, following the process shown in Exhibit 3.24.

The assumption here is that someone is calling out numbers continuously, or at least as fast as the recorder can write them down. Assuming that one number per second is recorded, the recording capacity will be 60 bubbles per minute.

The capacity for each department within the process is summarized as follows:

- Dipping: Capacity = 150
- Blowing: Capacity = 225
- Catching: Capacity = 12
- Measuring: Capacity = 45
- Recording: Capacity = 60

EXHIBIT 3.22 *Bubble-Catching Process*

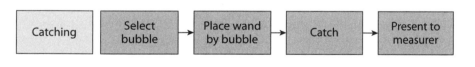

EXHIBIT 3.23 *Bubble-Measuring Process*

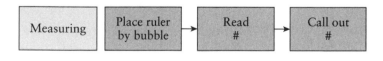

EXHIBIT 3.24 *Bubble-Recording Process*

This data show the capacity of each department in isolation. Because these departments are linked cross-functionally in the process, however, this isn't a realistic way to look at it. Taking the big-picture view of the process, it is evident that the overall capacity is really only 12 bubbles. It doesn't matter how many can be dipped or how many can be blown; all that matters is how many can be caught. If you actually conduct the demo, it will be obvious that this is the case. Bubbles will be hitting the floor because the catcher can't keep up, and the measurer and recorder will be idle for much of the time waiting for the catch. Therefore, catching is known as the *constraint*.

It is a common saying that a chain is only as strong as its weakest link. This is analogous to saying that a process is only as productive as its constraint. An important corollary is that to increase the strength of the chain, it is only necessary to strengthen the weakest link. Increasing process performance is therefore accomplished by zeroing in on and improving the constraint. It follows that if the objective of the bubble production process is to increase volume, any meaningful solution has to be targeted toward the catch. This means that automating the bubble blowing won't help. It means that adding resources to dipping won't help. And it even means that a common sense solution like eliminating the duplicate inspection being conducted by both dipping and blowing won't help. Think about it: It is very likely that a typical organization would view the cross-functional map and realize it had two departments doing exactly the same thing. So they would in turn form a team between dipping and blowing, determine how to alter the process so the inspection would only be done once, train everyone in the new procedure, and the capacity would still be 12 bubbles. So the supposed *improvement* would add no value to the process whatsoever. In fact, it may damage profitability, because now dipping and blowing will be able to go even faster, resulting in wasted solution while more bubbles hit the floor because catching cannot keep up.

These kinds of common sense solutions are perfect illustrations of how many organizations go about process improvement exactly backward from the way they should. Many functionally focused organizations ask each department manager to submit a performance plan each year that describes what they will do to improve their part of the organization. In other words, the dipping department manager submits what he or she will do to improve the dipping process, the catching department manager submits what he or she will do to improve the catching process, and so forth. Companies often require action items, budget dollars, and great volumes of detail to substantiate the activities. The thinking appears to be that if each of five departments improves its performance 10%, the overall organization will get 50% better. But the bubbles example illustrates the fallacy of this thinking. In reality, improving the performance of each of five departments by 10% only improves performance by 10%. Catching is the only area in which improvement is meaningful, and in the other four out of five departments, time and resources are being consumed to no purpose.

The bubbles illustration was included to demonstrate a critical concept regarding how to determine which processes have strategic significance because of gaps. Your organization probably has 10,000 or more processes, but the good news is that you don't have to improve *all* of them. The ones with the strategic significance are the *catchers*, or *constraints*. It follows that one responsibility of the leadership team when it comes to process assessment is to identify and manage the processes that are the constraints in their organization.

One technique for accomplishing this is to use process maps to diagram work flows from a big-picture perspective. The facilitator should think about the main work flows within the organization. For example, a hotel might view its work flow as shown in Exhibit 3.25.

EXHIBIT 3.25 *Hotel Work Flow*

The recommended process for constraint identification in this case would be to get people together from each area and create a high-level cross-functional process map that illustrates swim lanes and handoffs just like the IBM Credit and bubbles examples did. So the hotel would have reservations agents, front desk personnel (to provide feedback on both check-in and check-out), dining room staff, and housekeepers to cover the five main areas from left to right.

It is important when conducting the mapping session that the facilitator not let the group get bogged down with too much detail. A good practice is to have each group describe its own process in a maximum of five steps. Sticking to this maximum enables the map to be drawn in a reasonably short period of time and will be useful for promoting discussion.

The purpose of mapping the process on such a high level is twofold. First, the objective is to try to identify constraints. This is generally much easier to do with the entire process in view. Brainstorming process problems (even with a cross-functional group of people) without the entire process in view tends to result in each functional area identifying problems *within* their area versus *between* areas. The other benefit of cross-functional mapping in this fashion is education. Typically even at this high level, there will be participants in the group who are not aware of how the other departments execute their portion of the process. A sample process map resulting from this exercise is shown in Exhibit 3.26.

The next step after completing the map is to discuss as a group where the problems arise. Looking at the entire map provides a better perspective on which problems are the most significant. This particular organization provides insurance to corporations as opposed to individuals, and the policy issuance step is a major headache. The information coming from underwriting is rarely complete, requiring investigative work prior to policy issuance. This means that at times coverage is actually bound with pricing based on incomplete information, giving rise to the possibility of unforeseen losses. Another potential problem spot was the selective use of risk engineering to do the risk analysis. There were no hard-and-fast guidelines to help underwriting determine when the specialized

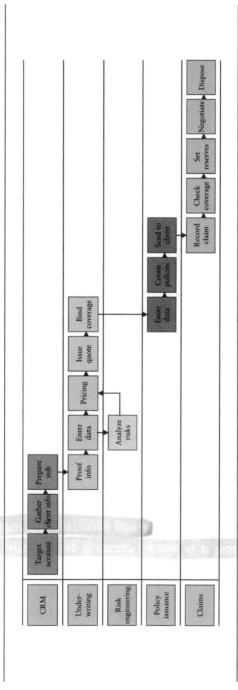

EXHIBIT 3.26 *Insurance Process Flow*

expertise was necessary. This caused the situation to evolve to a point where risk engineering was used if there was time for it, but skipped if there was not. This obviously is not the best criteria for making the determination of whether the analysis should be done. Some of the potential S.W.O.T.s resulting from this particular mapping session could therefore be:

- "Incomplete information from broker results in delays in quoting."
- "Incomplete information from underwriting results in (potentially very long) policy issuance delays."
- "Unrealistic deadlines encourage underwriting to skip risk engineering analysis, potentially resulting in an inaccurate quote."
- "Process for procuring risk analysis is not followed, potentially resulting in an inaccurate quote."
- "Poor data entry makes it difficult for claims to evaluate occurrences and begin the negotiation process."

Note that the first issue is broker-related and does not spring from any particular step on the flowchart. But it is common when discussing the cross-functional flow to have issues arise that impact the process that may not be specifically diagrammed. It is important to capture these issues when they arise, so this one is added to the list.

Diverse organizations may need to look at more than one cross-functional flow to enable a discussion of the key process constraints, but this shouldn't be an overly time-consuming part of the assessment. Remember that the important point when facilitating a mapping session is to surface key issues; it is *not* to create a technically perfect flowchart. Sometimes groups get bogged down trying to ensure they have the proper steps to the letter and that they haven't left out even the most minute detail. It is important to differentiate this exercise from a traditional improvement team–style process analysis. The map in this case is simply to open up a discussion of the key issues, so trying to be technically perfect is not an objective.

Identifying key process gaps is certainly important, but it is only one aspect of determining which processes have strategic significance. There also needs to be thought given to the positive side. In other words, what is the organization so good at that thought needs to be given to how to best capitalize on the capability? This gives rise to the next question on the template, which reads, "Which processes have strategic significance in terms of strengths and capabilities to be leveraged?" There are basically three different types of process-leveraging techniques to be considered: *process extension, market extension,* and *enterprise creation.*

Process extension deals with thinking about the different links on the value chain. Consider the diagram in Exhibit 3.27.

The diagram shows that each entity—supplier, your organization, and customer—has a series of process steps for which it is responsible. Process extension means thinking about ways to change the defined areas to assume more control over the process. In other words, it involves taking over one of the links in the chain from a customer or supplier because your organization can do it better. So the new flow could appear as shown in Exhibit 3.28.

This diagram shows the instance where your organization assumed responsibility for something that used to be the customer's responsibility. It must be noted that this should not be viewed as a confrontational

EXHIBIT 3.27 *Process Extension*

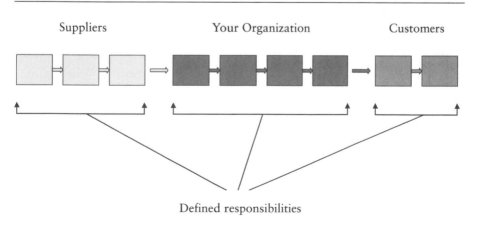

Suppliers   Your Organization   Customers

Defined responsibilities

EXHIBIT 3.28   *Process Extension*

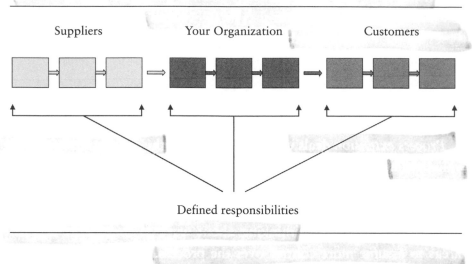

situation, or that your company is taking something away from your customers. Instead, it should be viewed as taking control of a process link because you have the capability to do it better and create a win-win situation.

A few examples might be useful in illustrating how process extension can work. A well-known company in the Midwest was responsible for building and delivering customized large machines to a Fortune 500 client base. The machines were expensive and complicated to build, and the 50,000-foot view of the process is illustrated in Exhibit 3.29.

So the process was really very simple: Suppliers would ensure that the relevant materials were available, and the machine-build organization would clarify the expectations of the customer, manufacture needed parts, assemble the machines, and ship to the customer. When a machine arrived on the customer site, the customer would unpack it, set it up, and start using it in their factories.

It seems straightforward, but there was a major recurring process problem: Customers would routinely damage the machine when setting it up. Because they were using technicians and maintenance people who had little experience with the new machines, it resulted in higher warranty claims, lower customer satisfaction, and endless finger-pointing between the customer and the machine-build representatives over whose fault it was that the machine wasn't functioning as advertised. More often than not, the machine-build company had to send a representative to the customer site to patch up both the machine and the relationship.

The solution was a classic case of process extension. The company decided to send a technician with the machine to each customer site. The technician would lead the efforts to unpack and set up the machine to get it ready for use. In other words, they changed the process boundaries as shown in Exhibit 3.30.

The benefits of the new process were numerous. Travel and personnel cost remained relatively flat, since most jobs required a technician to visit a customer site eventually anyway (and in the old process the visits were usually longer while the technician diagnosed and fixed all the problems). The solution was viewed as a big plus by the customer. Because the machine was ready to use faster, the technician could demonstrate features, answer questions, and spend more time with the customer in a non-confrontational manner. This resulted in large gains in customer

EXHIBIT 3.29 *Machine-Build Process Extension Example: Before*

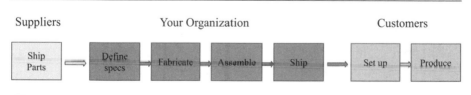

EXHIBIT 3.30 *Machine-Build Process Extension Example: After*

satisfaction, and increased the productivity of the machine so the customer could justify the expense more quickly.

A second example of process extension comes from Enterprise Rent-a-Car. If you were to ask a group of people who the biggest rental car company is, the answer will inevitably be Hertz. And who is number two? Avis. Continuing with this line of questioning will get people to list National, Budget, Alamo, Thrifty, Dollar, and so on. Most people will list six or seven companies before they think of Enterprise, if they think of Enterprise at all. But Enterprise took over as the largest car rental agency in the country several years ago and has remained so, with a 35.5% market share in 2004.

Why has Enterprise been so successful? Because they extended the boundaries of the car rental process. Before Enterprise, most car rental locations could be found at airports. To be sure, this is a time when people frequently need cars. But Enterprise reasoned that there were times when people would need a rental car other than when they were at an airport. This usually happens when their own automobile has been wrecked or is in the shop, which also happens to be the one time when they cannot go pick up a rental car. So Enterprise came up with the common sense solution of going to pick the customer up. This enabled them to access an entirely different customer segment with different sets of needs than the traveler segment that was always fought over by the industry. Enterprise set up relationships with large auto dealers, insurance companies, and automotive repair companies to help ensure that any vehicle rented at an off-airport location would be an Enterprise vehicle. They made things easier for the customers not only by picking them up, but also by dealing with the insurance aspect of car rental so customers wouldn't need to. And they have created and dominated a market in such a way that now the airport-focused organizations like Hertz realize the potential and are trying to play catch-up.

Just to be clear: The Enterprise example really shows two instances of process extension. The first deals with the transfer of vehicle from car rental company to renter. Enterprise assumed control of this link from the customer by going to pick the customer up. The second illustration of process extension is in the insurance portion of the process. The customer used to have to deal with this, but Enterprise assumed control over it. Note that in both instances win-win situations were created. Enterprise benefited in the first case because the access to a huge new customer segment drove sales, and the customer benefited because of the improved ease of finding transportation. The insurance portion of the deal was easier for Enterprise to negotiate and navigate because they have experience and the muscle that comes with large volumes of business, and the customer was relieved of dealing with a headache in a time when they are often distraught to begin with.

Another process extension example comes from General Electric. GE does pretty much everything, from making appliances and jet engines to providing insurance and loans. One of their best-known divisions is the appliance division. Many years ago, GE made the appliances and sold them through a network of small, medium, and large distributors. The large ones had no problem keeping the entire GE product line stocked, on the shelves, and in full view of potential customers, but the smaller distributors were having a problem. The inventory carrying costs of the full product line were too high to justify keeping everything in inventory on site. As a result, these distributors were only stocking certain appliances, causing GE to lose potential sales.

The process extension solution: GE took over inventory management from the small distributors. They set up central warehouses in large cities and agreed to let the smaller distributors order right out of the central stock, conditioned upon the agreement that the distributors keep the full GE product in sight for prospects to view. In this way, GE added inventory carrying cost versus the old system of passing it on to the distributors sooner, but this was more than offset by the additional sales brought in by increased exposure of the product lines. And distributors benefited from reduced carrying cost and increased sales potential. Again, this qualifies as a win-win solution. (Actually, since the customer also benefited from easier access to more products, this was a win-win-win solution!)

A final process extension example is an internal one, meant to show that there are many different applications of this line of thinking. A common internal customer–supplier relationship is that between IT and the rest of operations. This is an interesting example because, as was noted in the system mapping section, support functions often have the same groups serving as both customer and supplier to their portion of the organization. This relationship is illustrated in Exhibit 3.31.

It is commonplace in most organizations for operational areas to make project requests of IT. Upon receiving the request, IT ranks it relative to other priorities, then eventually develops and delivers the finished product or service for the requesting area to use. This process seems so simple, but in most organizations there are significant recurring problems. Often IT and operations do not speak the same language; IT doesn't understand the true problems operations faces, and operations has no idea what technology is available or what is or is not possible. The result is often unmet expectations; operations makes a request that IT cannot possibly deliver on, and then IT is perceived as aloof and uncaring when they do not deliver.

This is a potential example of process extension because miscommunication usually begins when IT receives the request. There is typically some sort of form for the requesting department to fill out that specifies exactly what IT is being asked to do. This form requires operations to fill in a lot of details that are critical to IT, but that operations may not truly understand the significance of. And even if operations *does* understand the significance, they often do not understand the technical details well enough to complete the form properly. This starts a negative chain reaction. IT gets an incomplete or misleading form, so they misunderstand the importance or relevance of the project. This can cause critical projects

EXHIBIT 3.31 *Internal Process Extension: IT Project Requests*

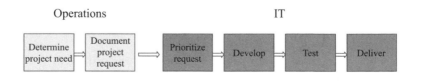

to be improperly prioritized and force them to wait in the queue while less important projects are completed. Even more seriously, it results in completed projects that do not meet customer expectations because of misunderstanding from the beginning.

The process extension solution, then, is simply to expand IT's responsibility within the process as shown in Exhibit 3.32.

By assuming control of the documentation step in the process, IT can solve a lot of problems. First, sitting with the operations person making the project request enables IT to understand exactly what is being requested. This obviously can help set realistic expectations for the operating group making the request (in other words, it can provide good *feed forward*, discussed in the system map section). Second, IT can ensure that all the technical details of filling out the request form are attended to, saving time and potential rework later in the process. Finally, it can break down barriers between departments resulting from lack of communication and create more of a team atmosphere. This almost certainly would lead to a higher level of customer satisfaction. Once again, process extension results in a win-win situation for the organization: less rework, lower cost, better results, increased productivity, and higher satisfaction level.

In terms of strategic assessment, it is recommended that a facilitator conduct a brainstorming session specifically to try to identify process extension applications. The best way to conduct this exercise is to describe what process extension is, provide several examples, and then give the participants a chance to think about possible company examples. From

EXHIBIT 3.32 *Internal Process Extension: IT Project Requests*

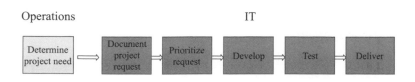

a technique perspective, it is important to have a session focused *solely* on process extension. If any other techniques are mixed in, it will dilute the focus on this type of process leveraging opportunity.

The second type of process leveraging technique is known as *market extension*. This involves attaining a high level of process proficiency in a certain segment in a market, then using the proficiency to attack another segment within the market. A classic example of this technique is Progressive Insurance. For many years, Progressive was known as a company that catered to the high-risk driver; if you were a Progressive customer, it was a fair bet that you had more than a few blemishes on your driving record. The entire auto insurance market could be represented as shown in Exhibit 3.33.

Progressive specialized in the high risk, segment. The instructive fact is that there is not as much traffic (no pun intended) in this segment. The only way to achieve long-term profitability is to maintain excellent process performance in underwriting, policy issuance, claims, and so on. Progressive's process performance was so good that they began to build reserves at a rate that gave them the capability to take on the giants of the industry in the medium-risk segment. And again, the proficiency in the key processes generated significant returns. (*Note:* Progressive is also a good example of process extension. In addition to the excellence in traditional insurance functions, they have extended their control over process links to include brokering. Indeed, a whole series of advertisements was built around the theme, "We may not have the lowest price, but we can tell you who does.".)

EXHIBIT 3.33　*Market Extension: Automobile Insurance Example*

Market Segments	High-Risk Drivers
	Medium-Risk Drivers
	Low-Risk Drivers

Another example of market extension comes from Nypro. The company specializes in injection molding and has been in business for over 50 years. Up until about the mid-1980s, the company was known as a player in the low-precision injection molding market, making toys and so forth. An aggressive approach to process improvement upgraded the company's ability to produce higher-precision injection molding products, enabling them to attack new market segments such as medical devices and computer chips. This transformed the company from $65 million in sales in the mid-1980s to over $700 million in 2005.

Again, the best technique for discovering potential market extension opportunities during strategic assessment is to describe the technique, provide the participants with a few examples, then ask for potential company applications. It is common when brainstorming potential examples to hear items that are technically more process extension than market extension. The facilitator should keep in mind that if a good idea surfaces under the "wrong" technique, the most important thing is simply to add it to the list anyway. As in the rest of the assessment, the objective is to identify all of the key S.W.O.T.s, not to develop a technically perfect list of market extension possibilities.

The final form of process leveraging technique is also the most aggressive. It is called *enterprise creation.* Enterprise creation is using the capabilities of a process to drive an entire new business or strategic direction for the organization. A classic example of this is H&R Block. The organization is best known for providing income tax preparation services. It only takes a moment of thought to realize that managing the work flow in a tax prep firm would be a tremendous challenge. The volume of work builds up to a tidal wave approaching the April 15 filing deadline, then drops off severely. The only way to manage this shifting level is to recruit, hire, and train employees in the "H&R Block way," bring them in to help process the avalanche of work, and then let them go.

The company developed a very high proficiency level in the recruiting, hiring, and training processes. So much so, in fact, that it enabled them to use the proficiency to drive strategic direction. Proficiency in these particular processes paved the way to doing them for others. Since these three processes are the cornerstones of what a temp agency would do, H&R Block opened temp service agencies throughout the country. Therefore, the process excellence enabled them to create an entirely new profit center.

Another excellent example of enterprise creation comes from L.L. Bean. The company is known for its sales of outdoor wear, primarily through its catalogs. This method of transaction necessitated that the company become proficient at call center processes. The company added centers in 1985, 1988, 1997, and 2004. The expertise in this area grew to the point that the management team realized that selling this capacity to other businesses could create an additional revenue stream. This is part of the reason the company has grown into a billion-dollar enterprise.

Ideas for enterprise creation are not restricted to the private sector. When brainstorming potential applications for a state Department of Management several years ago, an idea came up concerning the new state recycling contract. One of the existing responsibilities of the Department at the time was to deliver mail to all the government locations in the state. This necessitated that the Department of Management have the logistical expertise to move things around among all the state buildings. When the subject of enterprise creation came up, one of the participants mentioned that the state was in the process of sending the new recycling contract out to bid to the private sector. The idea was forwarded that since the logistical infrastructure was already in place, it would be possible to leverage this capability to move recycled materials just as easily as they moved the mail. Since the department is obviously a not-for-profit organization, this could save millions of dollars versus what the private sector would charge.

One of the strangest examples of enterprise creation came from a small not-for-profit physical rehabilitation clinic in the Midwest. The clinic, like many small organizations, was having trouble getting its managers to properly complete the performance appraisal process. Annual reviews were being done poorly (if at all), the forms were borrowed from a larger organization and were overly complex, and the managers saw no incentive to do the reviews since compensation wasn't based on them. The senior leadership felt that it was necessary for long-term development to conduct the reviews, so the clinic created performance appraisal software to make it easier for the managers to complete them. The software was interactive and walked each manager through a set of questions to help analyze performance. The product was a professional-looking printout to review with the employees. It was so much easier to use than the prior process that the managers loved it, and this fulfilled senior management's need to formalize the career development path.

The story could have ended here and been a nice example of process improvement, but there is much more. One day a visitor from a local business was in the clinic office and happened to see an acquaintance completing an appraisal on the computer. Noticing the software, the visitor remarked that it looked great and asked where the clinic purchased it. Upon being told that it was internally developed, the visitor asked how much they would charge to sell it to his organization. This spurred a huddle of the management team to determine a fair price, since selling it wasn't something they had even thought about. To make a long story short, word got out locally about the software. Several companies wanted to purchase it from the clinic. Demand grew to the point where it became a revenue source for the organization. A hybrid physical rehabilitation clinic and performance appraisal software developer certainly doesn't seem like a logical match. While it is true that the company sort of stumbled into this opportunity versus driving it from within, it is an excellent example of how process capability can be leveraged to drive totally new enterprises.

There is an important point to make about all three process leveraging techniques: a company will not typically find them unless it looks for them. In other words, specific time needs to be dedicated to trying to identify examples of each type. Most organizations get so tied up in trying to fix problems that they never really think about how to leverage process strengths. That is why any complete strategic assessment needs to include a session on these techniques. As has been noted, it is important to conduct these sessions in series rather than in parallel. In other words, it is improper technique to explain all of the techniques at once and then ask for examples. It is much better to explain one technique, provide examples, then give the group adequate time to think of company examples before moving on to the next category.

The strategic template lists the *process proficiency matrix* as a tool to use to help answer the question about devising S.W.O.T.s from process-based opportunities. The matrix is really just a form to help you record and organize ideas. A sample is shown in Exhibit 3.34.

To complete the matrix, it is customary to list the name of the process to be leveraged in the left-hand column. The second column is for proficiency class. The primary purpose of this column is to get the participants thinking about how the performance of the organizational process compares to competition within and outside of their industry. Recommendations for categories are as follows:

- WC = world class; best anywhere regardless of industry
- IC = best in the industry; has a competitive advantage
- AV = average; can compete within industry
- NI = needs improvement; noticeable gaps
- WW = world's worst; update your resumes

The *world class* category examples are typically candidates for enterprise creation. If a company has developed a capability to the point where it is world class, it is critical from a strategic perspective to determine how to best leverage the strength. The H&R Block hiring process

EXHIBIT 3.34 *Process Proficiency Matrix*

Process	Proficiency Class	Candidate for...			Comments
		Process Extension	Market Extension	Enterprise Creation	

is a classic example of a world-class process because it extended beyond the boundaries of the tax preparation industry to present an enterprise creation opportunity.

Industry class examples are typically candidates for market extension. Consider excess liability insurance carriers. Excess liability means that the organization only gets involved in paying a claim if something *really* bad happens! For example, a Fortune 500 company may need $150 million in liability insurance coverage. One insurer might provide $100 million in coverage with a $5 million deductible, or something of that nature. Then the excess liability carrier will provide coverage from $100 million to $150 million. So if a claim is for $125 million, the excess liability carrier would pay the amount over $100 million, which obviously would be $25 million. But the good news for the carrier is that a claim of $98 million would cost them nothing, as this is below the $100 million "attachment point."

Anyway, the point is that the customers of a company like this will only be organizations large enough to need $150 million (or more) in liability coverage. This means that medium and small organizations are not attractive prospects. However, one of the key tasks done when pricing excess liability policies is risk assessment, typically conducted by highly trained engineers. This expertise is obviously valued by the company because it enables them to give accurate (profitable) pricing. But it is also valued by the customer since during the analysis the engineers often identify things that the company can do in terms of preventative measures to reduce the probability of a large claim occurring at all. While medium and small companies may not need the *coverage* on a grand scale, they could benefit significantly from the *expertise* provided by the engineering team. The company could enter the medium and small market segments and sell the risk engineering services for a fee, leveraging its expertise and generating fees for the organization.

Any proficiency class may generate process extension examples. Extension may happen because an organization is very good at what it does and it is obvious that assuming control over more links in the process would be beneficial, as in the machine build example previously offered. It is also possible that extension would be necessary to close a gap. For example, consider the medical industry in Houston. There are many huge hospitals in the area, and several are growing. As a result, there is a shortage of qualified candidates to fill positions. One of the most difficult positions to hire for is that of nurse. Most qualified nurses already have good positions, so hiring is a difficult process. This particular hospital compounded the problem by having a difficult process for engaging and interacting with search firms that specialized in hiring for the medical profession. So the proficiency class was definitely *needs improvement*. The process extension solution was simply to purchase a search firm to do the hiring for them. This helped them bring the expertise in-house and have specialists on staff who were close to both the marketplace and the needs of the hospital.

Another process extension example comes from a situation with a serious gap. The proficiency class *world's worst* is listed tongue in cheek, but the point of phrasing it so bluntly is to alert the organization that something needs to be done right away to close the gap. For example, many financial services organizations set up offices abroad in places like Bermuda or the Cayman Islands to capitalize on favorable tax laws. But in order to reap the benefits of the tax advantages, it is sometimes necessary to jump through legal hoops. For example, a Bermuda-based insurance company may have to do business with Bermuda brokers, who in turn do business with U.S. brokers, who in turn do business with U.S. clients. This does two things: It ensures that the carrier conducts business in Bermuda under Bermuda tax laws instead of in the United States under U.S. tax laws, which could save the company millions of dollars. Unfortunately, it also isolates the company from its customer base, potentially leaving them out of touch with their customers' changing needs. This also puts them at the whim of the intermediate links. Should a U.S. or Bermuda broker make a mistake or communicate poorly, it is easier to tell the client that the carrier is to blame. This is an untenable position for the carriers because they cannot adequately defend themselves, since too much contact could run them afoul of the tax laws.

This is a case in which it would be natural to label the product/service delivery process as *world's worst*. It would be difficult to imagine a situation in which the customers and their specific needs were so difficult to determine by the supplying company. Because these needs are so difficult to determine, it makes it that much tougher to meet them. From a strategy perspective, some type of analysis needs to be done to evaluate whether giving up the tax advantages would bring in enough business and help avoid enough losses to justify the move. This definitely needs to be an item on the S.W.O.T. list.

The examples presented for the various proficiency categories are listed in the proficiency matrix in Exhibit 3.35.

Note that the comments section in the right-hand column is used to describe the problem or the process opportunity. These only need to be reworded slightly to turn them into properly written S.W.O.T.s, as follows:

- "Develop temporary agency business to leverage expertise in recruiting, hiring, and training."
- "Offer risk engineering consulting to non–Fortune 500 companies for a fee to generate risk-free income."
- "Send a technician to the customer site when shipping a machine to aid in setup, reducing warranty costs and getting the machine running faster."
- "Buy a search firm to locate hard-to-find categories of employee, ensuring that we will always have sufficient in-house expertise."
- "Geographic isolation from customers puts us out of touch with their needs and forces an over-reliance on the brokers."

The workshops and focus groups utilized to determine process leveraging examples are often the most interesting and enlightening portion of the assessment. They force participants to think about issues that otherwise will not be thought of.

The final strategic question from the process section of the template deals with the product/service offering. The overarching question is

Exhibit 3.35   *Completed Process Proficiency Matrix*

Process	Proficiency Class	Candidate for...			Comments
		Process Extension	Market Extension	Enterprise Creation	
Hiring (tax prep firm)	WC			Yes	Could develop temporary agency business to leverage process strength
Product delivery (insurance)	IC		Yes		Engineers known for their expertise; could offer risk consulting to small companies for a fee
Set up process (machine-build)	AV	Yes			Sending a technician to aid in setup could reduce warranty costs and get machine running faster
Hiring (hospital)	NI	Yes			Thin labor pool, competitive market. Could buy a search firm so we own the process
Product delivery (insurance)	WW	Yes			Isolated from customers and need to bridge geographic divide

straightforward: "What are the strengths and weaknesses of our product offering?" There are several issues to be discussed in making this determination, These are presented in the form of questions in the *product worksheet* shown in Exhibit 3.36.

The first question directs the user to list the main products that are considered to be competitors of the product your company wants to analyze. For example, Dell might want to evaluate a certain type of laptop computer against similar products from Gateway, Compaq, IBM, Sony, and so on.

Questions two and three are centered around the comparison between your product and competitors' products. Why do customers buy from you instead of the competition? Or why do they buy from the competition instead of you? Consider the example of a youth basketball organization that was looking to purchase T-shirts for all the players that participated in their tournament. The two choices for a vendor were Haynes and Gildan. The Haynes product was lighter, which could be desirable on hot days. There also was a bigger color selection to choose from, and the turnaround time for delivery was quicker. On the other hand, the Gildan product felt heavier (making it seem of better

EXHIBIT 3.36   *Product Worksheet*

Product: _____	Answers
1. What competitive products are on the market	a) b) c) d)
2. What features of this product make it superior to each competitive product?	a) b) c) d)
3. What features of each competitive product make it superior to ours?	a) b) c) d)
4. How long has this product been on the market?	
5. How long is a typical product life cycle?	
6. How long does it take for us to develop the "next-generation" product?	
7. Is this development time slower than, equal to, or faster than our competitors?	
8. What customer needs does our product fill?	
9. How will these needs change in the future?	
10. How do we gather customer information to ensure we can identify and adapt to changing needs?	
11. How does the reputation of the company enhance or hinder product perception?	

quality), was less expensive, and had an appealing collar style that the other choice did not have. Either organization could get value out of completing the product comparison of questions two and three to determine what the key S.W.O.T.s might be.

The next few questions deal with product maturity and the ability to innovate and turn out the next-generation product. Question four asks how long the product has been on the market, and question five is about the typical life cycle. Think about the technology of personal computers and how fast the definition of "state of the art" changes. Technological advances continue to make computers better, faster, more powerful, smaller, lighter, and so on. Conservative estimates would put the length of time a product could remain on the market and be 'cutting edge' at around six months. If the product being evaluated has been on the market for five months, it is obviously time to question how long it will remain viable. Question six probes further into the product development process, asking how long it takes to turn out the new and improved version of a product. If a product has a six-month product life cycle and a year-long product development cycle time, the company would obviously be in a precarious position. Predicting the ideal product two cycles forward would be very difficult (at least with any consistency). Question seven completes the analysis of the development process by asking if the company development time is faster than, slower than, or about the same as the competition. In a quick-moving industry, having a development time slower than competitors is certainly a competitive disadvantage.

The next questions are of a big-picture nature. Question eight asks what needs the product fills. For example, a cell phone fills the need for mobile communication, access to emergency services personnel, and other needs. The follow-up question then asks how these needs might change in the future. In the case of cell phones, recent features added include the ability to take photographs, send and receive e-mails, play music, and other features. This enhances the access and mobility element that customers value. It can be instructive to think about what features could be added to continue to meet and exceed expectations in the future.

Question ten asks how customer information is gathered to ensure that changing needs can be identified so the organization can adapt. It is important not to base all new product development or analysis of customer needs on opinion or gut instinct. Intuition, instinct, and experience are certainly important to new product development, but only *in conjunction with* data collection.

The final question asks how the reputation of the company enhances or hinders the perception of the product. This can identify potential barriers or advantages that need to be included in the S.W.O.T. list. For example, one of the newer models of automobile is the Mini Cooper. If you didn't know the manufacturer of the car, then you would have *no* preconceived notions about process quality. On the other hand, if you knew that the car was made by a company like BMW, you would have certain expectations. Volvo might create a different set, as would Yugo. Because Volvo is known for safety, any car coming from that organization would carry the assumption that it is safe. BMW carries the expectation of being expensive, well built, and fun to drive. Yugo was a very inexpensive vehicle not known for exceptional durability. Note that the perceptions of the various companies had no bearing on the actual quality of the Mini Cooper; it simply illustrates that the company reputation may dramatically affect the perception of its product, regardless of actual product quality. (Mini Cooper is made by BMW, by the way.)

A sample product worksheet is shown in Exhibit 3.37, using a comparison of one product to several different types of competing products.

There is nothing magical about the worksheet, but the questions are designed to help the organization think through its product positioning, and it may generate several critical S.W.O.T.s. For example, the previous worksheet could yield the following:

- "One county newspaper is aggressively trying to build circulation in its local market, resulting in a 27% drop in our circulation in that area in the last year."
- "Our writers are generally better than local papers, enhancing our reputation and leading to customer retention."

EXHIBIT 3.37   *Product Worksheet Example: Daily Newspaper*

Product: City Newspaper	Answers
1. What competitive products are on the market?	a) Internet b) Magazines c) County newspaper
2. What features of this product make it superior to each competitive product?	a) Local coupons, traditional medium, the "feel" of reading the paper b) More frequent information, more local information c) Better writing, more information, broader perspective
3. What features of competitive product make it superior to ours?	a) Real-time information, its free, younger generation grew up on it b) Better expertise, more in-depth analysis, name recognition c) More local information
4. How long has this product been on the market?	Paper has been published since 1925
5. How long is a typical product life cycle?	Indefinite, though new forms of information provision are eroding our market share
6. How long does it take for us to develop the "next-generation" product?	Not applicable in a traditional sense, though we do have an online version of the paper today
7. Is this development time slower than, equal to, or faster than our competitors?	The same as the county paper, but not applicable to the other forms of media
8. What customer needs does our product fill?	The need to be informed
9. How will these needs change?	Customers will continue to put a premium on convenience, and technology makes information flow much easier electronically
10. How do we gather customer information to ensure we can identify and adapt to changing needs?	Web surveys and informally
11. How does the reputation of the company enhance or hinder product perception?	Reputation is a positive with older customers because we have reliable delivery and have been around forever. Younger customers are more Internet-focused and the reputation isn't a factor

- "The Internet provides up-to-the-minute information to our customers, decreasing reliance on and demand for the paper."
- "Advertising rates are based on circulation numbers, and the introduction of new forms of media will erode our numbers and drive rates down."
- "Customers perceive the Internet gives them free access to information, so they don't see the need to spend extra on the newspaper."
- "Customers go to work earlier and earlier in today's business world, not leaving time to read the paper in the morning."
- "Our Internet product enables us to compete with other real-time sites and keep customers conditioned to look to us for their information."
- "Putting our product online has caused circulation to go down, because customers don't see the need to buy a paper when they can get the same information online for free."
- "Many customers like to read the paper while they eat breakfast, which is something they cannot conveniently replace with a computer terminal."
- "Our biggest customer segment is the long-term people who grew up reading the paper every day and aren't that familiar with the Internet; circulation will drop if we cannot profitably attract younger customers."
- "Coupons defray the cost of the paper for the customer."
- "Most customer information is gathered through web surveys, which may not be reliable indicators of the needs and feelings of the entire customer population."
- "Continued reliance of society on technology will almost certainly negatively affect circulation numbers."

This is just a sampling of the ideas a good discussion of product positioning can promote.

Again, these questions, tools, and workshops presented should be viewed as a menu to pick from for the process assessment. Each organization has its own set of issues and challenges that will make the assessment process unique, but properly following the guidelines presented will deliver a set of process S.W.O.T.s from which the organization can build a solid plan. The remainder of the assessment sections to be discussed serve as a necessary supplement to the process assessment.

FINANCIAL ASSESSMENT: IMPLEMENTATION

The goal of *financial assessment* is straightforward: to assess the current position and think through what the numbers are predicting about the future. The template suggests an analysis of the key financial indicators and how they are trending. The purpose of this is to reinforce whether the organization is in a growth climate or a mature climate, which will dictate different strategic decisions. Brainstorming can be used for identifying key financial indicators, but practically all companies will already know what they are. Tools listed that will help analyze trends are run and control charts. A *run* chart is simply a tracking of data as it rises and falls over time, as shown in Exhibit 3.38.

This particular chart shows a sales level that is generally stable, or flat over time. There are many ups and downs, but no discernible long-term trends. This could mean many things. Perhaps the demand for the product or service the company makes has flattened out. Perhaps the campaigns designed to boost sales have not worked. Perhaps price increases (or decreases) were put in place that kept sales dollars flat but dramatically affected profitability. Any of these are possibilities. The instructive point here is that the chart can give you the foundation to build a hypothesis from, but it is up to the management team to use its knowledge to determine the true reason behind flat sales. This is an important concept because it illustrates one of the benefits of formal versus informal assessment. Informal assessment requires little data because everything is based on brainstorming. This puts the burden on the management team to do three things: (1) remember the topic of sales during brainstorming, (2) accurately remember the financial figures and trends, and (3) assign the proper cause to craft a well-written S.W.O.T. In the formal assessment, the first two issues will not be significant because the assessment

EXHIBIT 3.38 *Monthly Sales Run Chart*

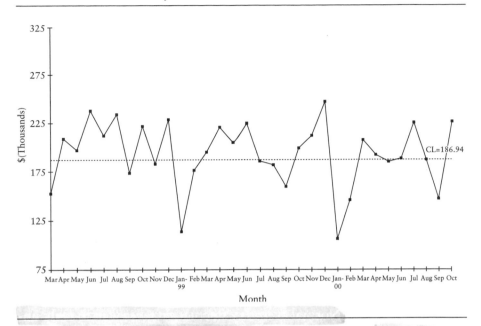

Month

process addresses them. Therefore, all the management team will need to do is assign the proper cause. This reinforces the notion that the formal assessment will yield a more comprehensive list of key S.W.O.T.s.

Control charts are also referenced as a potentially useful tool for data analysis. A control chart is simply a run chart with mathematically determined limits added. These limits differentiate the type of everyday variation that is built into the process from truly unusual events. A practical example may help illustrate this concept. Suppose your drive to work in the morning takes an average of 30 minutes. Sometimes it may take 35, sometimes it may take 25, but the average is about 30. Knowing this, what would you do if one day it took you 32 minutes to get there? You are two minutes above average, which in this case is a bad thing. Should you form a task force of your subordinates to walk the trail back to your house to determine where exactly the two-minute deviation occurred? This would obviously be an ineffective strategy, since you probably just caught an extra red light or there were a few more kids at the crosswalk than normal. By the time your task force walked the trail, those kids would be in their second period class and there would be nothing to find. (Which brings up another interesting point: Subordinates would never come back to the boss and say, "Gee, we have no idea why the deviation occurred." They would instead craft an explanation that may or may not have anything to do with reality. This could quite possibly be followed by a management decision based on their report that would send the company spinning off in an inappropriate direction.)

On the other hand, if one day the drive time was 120 minutes, would you consider *that* to be unusual? This would almost certainly be the case, and the interesting point is that you wouldn't need a task force to tell you why it happened. You would know it was because of the fifteen-car crash or the water main break or whatever. The point is that somewhere between the 30-minute average and the 120-minute extreme something happens: Normal everyday fluctuation gives way to truly unusual events. This boundary between common and special is important to understand, because it can impact your management decision making. Consider the control chart example in Exhibit 3.39.

EXHIBIT 3.39 *New Customer Sales Control Chart*

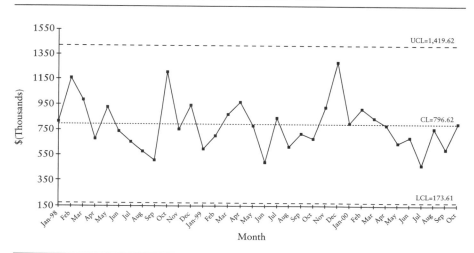

Note the similarities to the run chart. The only real difference is the presence of the UCL (Upper Control Limit) and LCL (Lower Control Limit) lines. These lines cannot simply be set wherever the user wants to set them. They are *calculated* based on actual historical data on the subject in question. The formulas for construction of the limits and theory behind them can be found in any elementary statistics book, but the important item for assessment purposes is the interpretation. The interpretation of Exhibit 3.39 tells us that, because everything is inside the limits with no discernible trends, new customer sales is basically steady over the course of time. Is this a good or a bad thing? It depends on the target for new customer sales. In this chart the organization averages just under $800,000 per month in new sales. If the target is $1,000,000 per month, then the organization is and will continue to be predictably lousy! Several potential S.W.O.T.s could result from this finding, including any or all of the following:

- "Insufficient sales to new customers threaten overall profitability."
- "Sales incentives aimed at new customer attraction have not successfully enabled us to meet our targets."
- "Sales force inexperience is preventing us from attracting sufficient new business."

On the other hand, consider the chart presented in Exhibit 3.40. This particular version has a point in December 1999 that is above the upper limit (UCL). This is typically referred to as a *special cause* situation. The appropriate course of action in this case is to investigate to determine the cause, which in this example could yield any of the following S.W.O.T.s:

- "Price cutting at 1999 year-end attracted new customers, but resulted in negative bottom-line impact that is threatening all new investment."
- "Sales development training conducted in November 1999 drove new customer acquisition higher than ever before."
- "Offer prospects long-term buying incentives to attempt to repeat the record acquisition at the end of 1999."

EXHIBIT **3.40**   *New Customer Sales, Version Two*

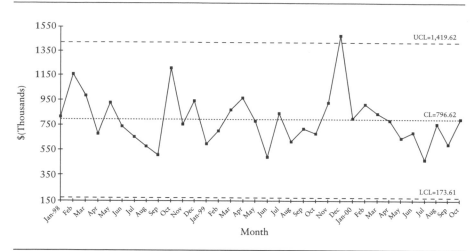

Once again, the chart gives valuable data regarding *what* happened, but the management team must use its knowledge and experience to determine *why* it happened and the implications of the event. Any of the three conclusions listed are plausible reasons for the spike on the graph; management must determine the *real* reason.

Control charts are not new tools invented for the purpose of strategic assessment. On the contrary, they have been used for various business applications dating all the way back to pre–World War II. Using them for trend identification and interpretation is sometimes very helpful during the assessment process, and not only for financial figures. It is common to see control charts used for tracking customer and process data as well. Using these charts to supplement other more traditional forms of financial analysis can yield good information for assessment purposes.

The next question posed on the financial assessment template is, "What external factors will impact our financials?" The purpose of this question is to get management to think about potential future financial issues; these types of things will not show up on charts filled with historical data. The tool/technique listed for this question is brainstorming, which could be supplemented by forecasting, dynamic financial analysis, or a host of other more sophisticated analytical techniques.

The final question under financial assessment deals with the budget that has been allocated to strategic plan execution. This is a critical question because many organizations do not link strategy and budget. Many times plans wither and die when initiatives resulting from plan development are not properly funded and the associated objectives are not met. Failure to allocate resources also creates the impression that strategy isn't that important, or that it is something to do only after your real work is done. The tool jokingly referred to as being useful to help answer the budget question is a sledgehammer. The point being made here is that it must be "hammered home" from the beginning of strategic plan development that the completion of the plan is the *starting point*, not the *finish line*. Many managers have a project mentality; once the plan is complete, they (consciously or subconsciously) cross it off their to-do list and move on to the next item. In reality, the work only begins once the plan is complete. Having budget dollars dedicated to execution is a must in order to reinforce the importance of the plan and give the organization a realistic chance to execute it effectively.

CUSTOMER ASSESSMENT: IMPLEMENTATION

The purpose of the *customer assessment* is to balance internal analysis with the external perspective. No assessment can truly be complete without considering the needs and direction of the marketplace. The questions and tools from the customer assessment are reprinted in Exhibit 3.41.

The first question deals with customer segmentation. There are a number of ways a company can segment its customer base (e.g., product type, size of customer, geographically). The objective is to isolate the different segments that are strategically important to meet the mission and vision, determine each segment's needs and expectations, and think about how those needs may change in the future.

EXHIBIT 3.41   *Customer Assessment Framework*

Key Questions	Potentially Useful Tools
Customer Assessment	
What are the key customer segments?	Brainstorming
What are the key S.W.O.T's surrounding relationships with key customer segments?	System maps
What "must be's" of the relationships are not met?	Kano analysis
What can we do to "delight" each segment?	Kano analysis
What are our key competitors' strengths and weaknesses?	Focus groups/customer research
How will the industry change in the future?	Focus groups/customer research

For example, consider a traditional U.S. airline. The segments of the airline might be business travelers, leisure travelers, and cargo shippers. The business traveler segment may put a premium on convenience and speed of travel. A business traveler might be willing to pay an extra few hundred dollars to travel from Dallas to Chicago if the flight leaves at their preferred time, is nonstop, and will get them there in time for their big meeting. A leisure traveler, however, may be far more interested in price. This person might be willing to leave at 6 a.m. and connect in Salt Lake City to get from Dallas to Chicago if it can be done cheaply.

The interesting thing about this example is that the same person can fit into both segments at different times. This illustrates the need for segmentation by customer type versus simply segmenting into passengers and cargo. The cargo segment may be further broken down into *high-volume* and *low-volume* shippers if the company feels that needs and expectations will vary between the two groups and each group needs to be analyzed.

Another segmentation example comes from the consulting business. Orion Development Group is one of the top consulting companies in the country, specializing in the fields of strategy development and process improvement. It has partnerships with universities throughout the United States, and a large portion of its business involves conducting public seminars through the universities. The *public seminar participants* are a key customer segment. These people receive one of the seminar brochures in the mail, decide that the topic would be of value, and register and attend the programs at the university. The need of this segment is transfer of information. The range of participants might be from those who know nothing about a topic to those who are practically experts, but they share the goal of learning more to determine whether and how to implement the chosen concepts in their own organizations.

The next segment consists of *in-house training customers*. These companies receive the brochure in the mail and decide that it would be of greater value to have an instructor come to the company and teach a group of internal people versus sending a person or two to a university to learn. This segment shares the public seminar participants' goal of knowledge transfer, but wants to discuss more of its own company examples and how the concepts specifically apply.

The third main customer segment is the *process consulting customers*. These companies have a specific process problem they need help in fixing. This involves having a consultant come on site to help with the mapping, determine process gaps, help identify, prioritize, and implement solutions, and so forth. In short, facilitate the entire process for fixing the problem.

The fourth and final segment for the company is the *strategic consulting customers*. These companies need assistance in the development of a strategic plan or Balanced Scorecard. While this segment shares many of the same characteristics as the process consulting customers (i.e., they need help finding a solution to a gap they are experiencing), the company chose to separate the strategic clients for a very important reason: the contact level within the customer's organization. Requests for process consulting can come from many different levels within the customer organization, depending on the size and complexity of the process in questions. Requests for development of strategic tools, however, almost always come from the company's executive team. Because of this, it is important that Orion have people handling these requests and conducting the engagements who have been executives and can relate to executives.

Once the appropriate customer segments have been defined, the company may proceed to question two from the assessment template: "What are the key S.W.O.T.s surrounding relationships with key customer segments?" Each segment the company considers to be of strategic importance (i.e., it will significantly impact their ability to meet the parameters established by the vision) can be analyzed via the system map tool introduced in the process assessment section. In this instance, the company as a whole should be placed in the P/D/C/I box and the customer segment placed in the oval as the answer to output question one. An airline example is shown in Exhibit 3.42.

The customer segment system maps raise a host of important issues for discussion. The box in the lower right-hand corner is an analysis of the key customers' needs and how well they are being met, both perceived and actual if data is collected. The feedback and feed forward questions tell how connected the company is to the customers, and the analysis of gap causes provides feedback on the internal processes and issues that cause the gap. This is valuable information in itself, but looking at the supplier side helps complete the picture. The box in the lower left-hand corner enables the company to evaluate its suppliers, again both perceived and actual if data is collected. The communication boxes are still present to evaluate interaction quality, and the gap analysis gives an indication of how much of the problem is internal versus external. Potential S.W.O.T.s that could come out of this exercise are as follows:

- "Scheduling department bases schedule on models versus real-world experience, resulting in overcrowding of hubs that leads to flight delays."
- "Frequent Flyer program is perceived by customers to be average at best, and certainly doesn't attract customers to the airline."
- "Heavy turnover among gate agents results in poorly trained staff dealing with customers and unmet expectation."

EXHIBIT 3.42 *Airline Customer System Map Example*

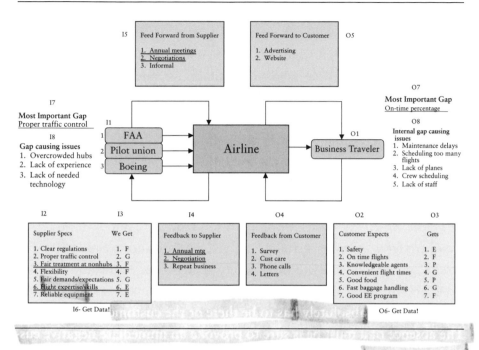

- "Cost pressures have reduced spare crew and plane availability, leading to more flight delays."
- "Cumbersome negotiation process prevents us from making midterm changes to the pilot contract, resulting in operational delays."
- "Pilot expertise is superb, contributing to an industry-best safety record."
- "Outdated flight control technology prevents controllers from optimizing traffic flow."
- "Food service is extremely poor on domestic flight, creating a window of opportunity for competitors."
- "Customers value our convenience when flying between major cities, leading to repeat business."

Does a company need to create a system map for every customer segment? Of course not. The objective is to determine which segments are the most important strategically and analyze them. There are usually about a half-dozen or less strategically important segments, so the system map analysis should take one to two days to effectively complete, pending data collection issues. The participants in the session should be a combination of people who understand customer needs with those who can pinpoint internal reasons for not meeting those needs. Collecting data to confirm or deny perceptions is a critical part of the analysis. An organization often perceives one set of needs to be critical, but the customer has a very different list of expectations. It would be appropriate to add a S.W.O.T. dealing with the lack of understanding of customer needs in this case.

The next two questions introduce terms that were popularized by the *Kano model of quality*, introduced by Noriachi Kano in the 1980s. The model holds that there are three levels of customer needs and satisfaction. The first and most basic is the "must be" level. A "must be" is something that absolutely has to be there or the customer will be upset. The absence of a must be is sure to provoke an immediate negative customer reaction. For example, consider a stay in a hotel. The list of items that would qualify as must be include a clean room, hot water, a bed, an electronic key that opens the door, a television, and so on. No matter what price a customer pays, almost any customer would consider these to be standard features.

An important feature of the *must be* category is that meeting all of them doesn't guarantee customer satisfaction or loyalty. Customers don't usually call their friends after a hotel stay and tell them, "I stayed in a great hotel this weekend—it had a bed! Right there *in the room*! You have to go check this place out!" In fact, a must be could be diagrammed as shown in Exhibit 3.43.

The vertical scale reflects customer satisfaction. The range is from a totally dissatisfied customer at the bottom to a completely satisfied customer at the top. The horizontal scale measures how well the particular characteristic has been fulfilled. The left-hand side of the scale indicates total lack of the characteristic in question, and the right-hand side reflects that the characteristic has been completely fulfilled.

EXHIBIT 3.43 *Kano Model of Quality: The "Must Be"*

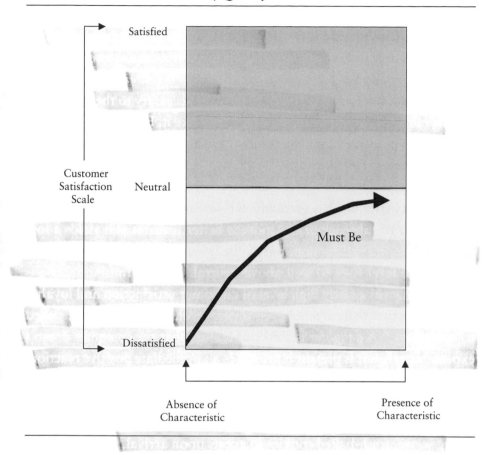

In the case of the *must be*, the line drawn on the model shows that the absence of the must be characteristics reflect a very dissatisfied customer, but as more and more must be's are met, the satisfaction level starts to rise. However, notice that the satisfaction never goes above neutral, reemphasizing the point that meeting the *must be* cannot result in a high level of customer satisfaction or loyalty. Meeting the must be's is just like the ticket to get into a movie; you have to have one to get in, but the ticket doesn't make going to the movies a memorable experience. Kano pointed out that so many organizations spend so much time just trying to satisfy the must be characteristics that they do not realize they are just meeting the minimum.

The moral of the story is that to create a high degree of customer satisfaction, it is necessary to move beyond the bare minimum level. The second level of customer satisfaction, called *more is better*, does just that. More is better features may not be absolutely necessary to the customers, but the more they see of them, the better they like it. For example, a towel in a hotel is a must be, but the bigger, thicker, and softer the towel is—more is better. A television might be a must be, but the capabilities of having cable, movie channels, on-demand movies, and video games is better. The more is better line has been added to the model in Exhibit 3.44.

Note that the absence of any more is better features still yields a low level of customer satisfaction, but as the more is better features become present, the level rises to well above neutral. Indeed, fulfilling more is better's can yield a fairly high level of customer satisfaction and loyalty.

Kano felt that there was an even higher level, however, and he called it "delighters." A *delighter* is a special feature that the customer doesn't expect, but when it is present it provokes an immediate positive reaction. A great example comes from Doubletree Hotels. If you ask a roomful of people what differentiates Doubletree from the other hotel chains, you will immediately hear "The cookies!" Many years ago, Doubletree began giving warm, fresh-baked cookies to guests upon arrival, and this simple feature continues to make a big impression. Another example comes from the Hotel DeVille in Binghamton, New York. A guest returned for a second visit six months after his initial stay, and was upgraded to a suite for no charge. Upon entering the room, he found a fruit basket and bottle of champagne with a note that read "Welcome back" with his name on it. This sort of thing might be expected when visiting the same hotel over and over, but for a two-time visitor, it made a huge impression. And there has never been an instance when this traveler has returned to Binghamton without staying in the Hotel DeVille.

Premium hotel chains (versus economy hotels) really have to go the extra mile to do something that qualifies as a true delighter. Here's an example from the Four Seasons that would certainly make the grade. A

EXHIBIT 3.44 *Kano Model of Quality: The "More Is Better"*

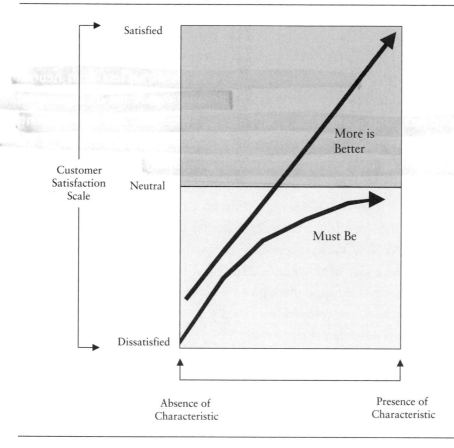

customer was checking out of a Four Seasons and told the desk clerk that he was very nervous because he was flying to New York to make a 2 p.m. presentation to over 400 people. He was so nervous, in fact, that he left his presentation materials in a briefcase right in front of the registration desk, and didn't discover the error until he was on his flight to New York. To his dismay, there was no chance of getting back to the hotel on time, so he had no choice but to make the best of it. At 1 p.m. he was busy lining up flipcharts on the stage side by side and putting large writing on them (trying to write large enough for 400 people to be able to see!), when the doorman from the hotel in his originating city walked in.

This gentleman had found the briefcase, driven to the airport, flown to New York, found the hotel, and delivered the training materials. This would almost certainly qualify as a delighter by any standards! The delighter line has been added to the model in Exhibit 3.45.

Note that the absence of delighters still yields no less than neutral with regard to customer satisfaction. Because customers do not expect delighters, they cannot be disappointed when they are not present. However, continuing to provide delighters to customers results in the highest rating for customer satisfaction and loyalty.

There are a number of important points to be made regarding Kano analysis. First, an alert observer would note that all the delighter examples given require additional cost. Whether it is a bottle of champagne or a flight to New York, it certainly is possible that a delighter will add to the expense side of the ledger. However, the goodwill and customer loyalty generated through these giveaways can more than offset the cost involved if they are deployed judiciously.

Remember also that if the strength of your company lies in developing strong customer relationships, identifying and implementing a delighter is not a one-time chore for you. As soon as a delighter is introduced, it quickly begins sliding down the scale toward must be. Think about the Doubletree example: a frequent guest at the hotel would be looking forward to receiving the cookies, and if they weren't there it would cause dissatisfaction. Even though other comparably priced chains don't have cookies, Doubletree has set the expectation and now must live up to it. Think about buying a new car. Things like CD players, automatic door locks, automatic windows, power steering, anti-lock brakes, air bags—all of these were considered delighters at one time, but today they are almost all seen as must be features. This phenomenon dictates that an organization must continue to come up with new and interesting delighters to keep its customers happy and loyal.

The phrasing of the last sentence was critical: the *company* must continue to come up with delighters. It is a mistake to rely on customers to tell you what would delight them; *your* organization must determine what delighters could be. Most customers don't understand your business well

EXHIBIT 3.45   *Kano Model of Quality: "Delighters"*

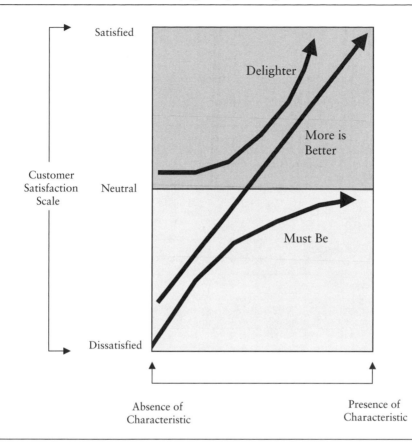

enough to even begin to know what you may be capable of providing. For purposes of strategic assessment, the two questions from the template are meant to determine what must be features are not being met and what delighters might be possible. It is recommended that a focus group be conducted with people within the organization to determine what issues fall in each category. The process should be as outlined in Exhibit 3.46.

Note that the delighters exercise is split into two categories. When trying to identify delighters, participants typically start with ideas that involve free giveaways. The delighter is that they should take the customer to the baseball game, out for dinner, to the golf course, and the

EXHIBIT 3.46 *Conducting the Kano Focus Group*

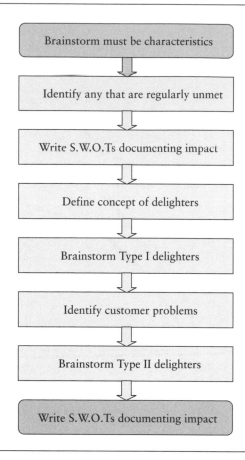

like. These are good relationship-building ideas, but they are not powerful competitive differentiators because they can be so easily matched by competitors.

A different and more lasting delighter can be found if the focus switches to solving customer problems. The facilitator should instruct the participants in the focus group to put themselves in their customers' shoes and think about the problems they face on a daily basis. This doesn't necessarily need to be problems with *your* company. The intent is to determine what causes your customers pain from *any* source. Once a list has been compiled, brainstorm ways in which your organization can solve their problems for them. Experience shows that ~~solving problems for customers~~ ~~that they are not expecting you to solve creates a long-lasting delighter.~~ The Machine build opportunity for process extension actually originated out of a Kano brainstorming exercise. The customer problem identified was that of damaging machines during the setup phase, leading to the process extension suggestion of sending the technician with the machine to assist.

Sample S.W.O.T.s that could come out of a Kano exercise are as follows, with must be violations followed by different types of delighter possibilities. The context of the example is for a hotel.

- "Electronic keys routinely do not unlock guestroom doors, resulting in return trips to the front desk and lower customer satisfaction."
- "Limited hot water during peak early morning hours results in customer complaints."
- "High turnover and insufficient staffing levels among the housekeeping staff results in some rooms not being cleaned until very late in the day, delaying check-in for new guests and inconveniencing existing guests."
- "Stock an umbrella in each guest room in the spring to prevent guests from getting wet during the rainy season."
- "Provide passes to the adjacent health club to premium guests, allowing them to get a first-rate workout for free."
- "Place fruit basket in the room of all returning guests, welcoming them back to the hotel."
- "Electronically transmit receipts to customers' e-mail address to aid in expense reporting."
- "Provide video conferencing capabilities in guest rooms so business guests can conduct meetings in private."

The Kano exercise is very useful in provoking thought and evaluating customer relationships in nontraditional ways.

The next customer assessment question involves identification of competitors' strengths and weaknesses. The potential tools listed to answer this question are focus groups and/or research. The organization must evaluate how much formal research is needed to determine the necessary level of competitive analysis. The product worksheet developed in the process assessment section provided an informal version of competitive product assessment; a similar thought process could apply to competitors. Many organizations conduct excellent formal research, so it would be up to the organization to decide how best to glean the necessary S.W.O.T.s for planning purposes.

The final customer assessment question is about the industry in general and how it will change in the future. Once again, the company must decide between focus groups and formal research to identify the necessary information. If the decision is made to use focus groups, a good process is to pick a time point in the future (five years out, ten years out, whatever the planning horizon happens to be). Ask what changes are going on in the industry and how they will transform the way business is conducted by the target date listed. It is instructive to think about technology, competitor consolidations, customer consolidations, the mutation of product and service offerings, and so forth. Upon completion of this focus group, the customer assessment questions will have been answered.

LEARNING AND GROWTH ASSESSMENT: IMPLEMENTATION

There are two purposes to the *learning and growth assessment*. One is to evaluate the support systems of the organization to determine how well they will be able to fuel process performance, customer satisfaction, and financial results. The other is to ensure that management takes a participative role in generating the S.W.O.T.s. This component can be essential to buy-in later in the process. The questions and tools used in the learning and growth assessment are reprinted in Exhibit 3.47.

The first question brings management opinion into the assessment. It is a good idea to schedule individual interviews that are approximately a half-hour in length for the senior leadership team. These interviews should consist of roughly half a dozen questions to start, and all should

EXHIBIT 3.47 *Learning and Growth Assessment Questions and Tools*

Key Questions	Potentially Useful Tools
Learning and Growth Assessment	
What does management think key S.W.O.T.'s are?	Management interviews
Does management have a consistent vision?	Management interviews
How high is morale, and what are the key influences?	Management interviews/ employee focus groups
Do employees understand the vision?	Employee focus groups/survey
Do employee agree with management on Q 1&3?	Employee focus groups/survey
What future technology changes will impact us?	Focus groups/research
How will needed workforce skills change in the future, and are we prepared to be successful in that environment?	Focus groups/research

be centered around the identification of S.W.O.T.s. Suggested interview questions include:

- What is the vision for the future? (Sales/revenue, key customer groups, number of employees, etc.)
- What are the top three strengths of the organization that will help us achieve this vision?
- What are the top three weaknesses of the organization that will prevent us from achieving this vision?
- What are the top opportunities you think we need to capitalize on to help us take steps toward the vision?
- What external threats may hamper our ability to meet the vision?
- How would you rate employee morale on a scale of 1 to 10 (10 being the best), and what factors contribute to the rating given?

Asking the vision question can be very revealing. The interviewee might need some prompting to give a usable answer. It is good to ask about an overall sales projection (if you are in a for-profit organization), because comparing the numbers given from executive to executive reveals how in tune they all are to the business. The same holds true if asking about customer needs and how they will be changing. Sometimes the range of answers makes it clear that certain members of the team are not really plugged in to the business. One assessment revealed that a few management team members could not even *identify* the external customers of the organization, much less discuss their needs. Having executives who are out of touch with customer needs is obviously not a healthy situation and definitely worthy of mention on the S.W.O.T. list.

The next four interview questions literally ask for management opinions in the four S.W.O.T. categories. The goal is not only to get feedback on the key issues, but also to determine whether management is consistent in their view of what the key issues are. For example, during one assessment the interviewer had eight executive team interviews to schedule. The first seven respondents all said that the number-one weakness of the organization was lack of trust and cooperation among the members of the management team. The eighth and last executive said that the number-one *strength* of the organization was management team cooperation and trust. After watching the group interaction during the assessment, it became obvious that the final executive was damaging relationships among all members and was the cause of the problem. While this may have been clear anyway, the interview process illustrated how problematic the situation had become.

The next question asks management to rank employee morale on a scale of 1 to 10 and discuss factors that influence their rating. Understanding the morale of the workforce is imperative to the assessment process. A company with high morale is far more adaptable to change than one with low morale. If the ranking is low and the causes are fixable, it would be a good idea to include the potential fixes as opportunities on the S.W.O.T list. If the causes are not fixable, they should be included as threats on the S.W.O.T list. In either case, it is important to assess the morale factor. Note that employee focus groups are listed as a potential tool for assessing morale in addition to management interviews. It is instructive to see whether employees have the same perception of morale that management does and whether the causative factors are consistent. Significant disparity in the perceptions of the two groups could indicate that management really doesn't understand or feel connected to their employees, which certainly should be added to the S.W.O.T. list.

A related employee focus group question is about the company vision. Many organizations have an employee group that understands the vision and lives it day to day, which is a powerful strength to have. In other organizations, the employees can quote vision verbatim, but it really doesn't mean anything to them or affect how they do their jobs. And still other organizations have employees who have no idea the company has a vision or even what a vision is for. Asking about the vision usually leads to a revealing discussion of how much ownership the employees have in company success and can certainly lead to the generation of many key issues for the list of S.W.O.T.s. Marked differences in management and employee perceptions on vision for the future should be noted as well.

The next learning and growth assessment question deals with future technology. It is typically useful to (either formally or informally) assess how technology will impact the organization and industry in the future. This can be done via focus groups or more formal research. Since technology is increasing the speed of business on almost a daily basis, it is imperative to spend time trying to determine relevant technology-focused S.W.O.T.s. If the chosen course is to use focus groups, it is a good idea to mix internal technology experts, operational people, and employees who are close to the customers' needs. This mix will enable you to discuss the technological capabilities that customers want, the capabilities that processes need, and the techno-trends that might result in filling all the gaps.

The final learning and growth assessment question is focused on the workforce skills necessary to be successful in the future. Being good at what you currently do is often not sufficient to guarantee future success. For example, many years ago there was certainly a company that was number one in its field of producing buggy whips for horse-drawn carriages. Being the best today is no guarantee of future success, however. No matter how cost efficient the company was or how wonderful its product was, it became irrelevant when people started traveling by car and didn't need buggy whips any more. Therefore, the long-developed skills of the employees in whip production eventually became irrelevant.

A more recent example comes from a state Treasury Department. Tax returns in the state had always been processed manually, so having an army of reviewers on staff possessing a certain set of skills was required. But due to resource constraints, the state began a big push toward electronic filing. The skills needed to succeed in this environment were obviously much more technology-oriented, so the current skills could be at odds with necessary future skills. Identifying whether skills needed for the future are present in the current workforce is the final critical element for the S.W.O.T. list.

SUMMARY

It is important to remember that the questions posed in the template should be viewed as a menu; not all of them will be ordered in every situation. When conducting an assessment of any individual organization, certain questions may be excluded and additional questions added. It is necessary to keep the overall intent in mind: identifying the key issues that will impact the ability to meet the parameters established by the organizational vision. Once the assessment has been completed, the organization will be ready to take the S.W.O.T.s generated and move to the next step: building a *strategy map*.

CHAPTER 4

STRATEGY MAPS

The *strategy map* is a tool popularized by Robert Kaplan and David Norton in their series of *Harvard Business Review* articles and books focused on strategy and the Balanced Scorecard. The map is the next step in the strategic process, taking all the data gathered during the strategic assessment and using it to develop a one-page blueprint that articulates the strategy of the organization. In this chapter the definition, development, and utilization of the map will be presented.

DEFINITION

A *strategy map* is a tool that enables an organization to articulate its strategy through a series of cross-functional cause-and-effect relationships. There are several important concepts embedded in the definition. The first is the idea that the map helps *articulate* strategy. Many organizations have a strategic plan thick enough to resemble an encyclopedia. Giving this plan to a stakeholder (e.g., manager, employee, board member, customer) to help them understand the direction of the company is a fruitless exercise. It is extremely difficult to understand such a document unless the stakeholder has tremendous interest, a thorough appetite for detail, and a lot of time on their hands. The strategy map, however, clearly illustrates the main strategic themes of the organization and how they are linked together. This enables the organization to effectively tell the story of its strategy in a relatively short period of time.

Another key element of the definition is the cross-functional aspect. Many organizations develop strategy in pieces; the sales department develops a forecast, the operations people develop ideas to make processes more efficient, finance develops the budget, human resources develops a training plan, and so on. Then it is all cobbled together and called a strategy. Upon reading a client company's strategic plan, an external consultant commented that, "I am clearly the only person who has ever read this plan from cover to cover." When asked why, he explained that not only were the writing styles dramatically different, but there were several points where the plan contradicted itself. There were also identical initiatives identified and explained in multiple places, illustrating that the authors were unaware of what the other authors had already covered.

The impact of this situation is that each functional area within the company would attempt to execute its portion of the plan independently, which may or may not be effective. The job of senior management is to make all of the pieces work together, not try to optimize each piece at the possible expense of the whole. The strategy map provides the perfect vehicle for illustrating how all of the different pieces should fit together and support each other. So instead of human resources developing a training plan in isolation, for example, the specific operational needs driven by the training will be highlighted on the map. The relationships between operational efficiency, customer satisfaction, and financial return will be illustrated on the map as well.

The third key element of the definition is the cause-and-effect relationship between strategic objectives. Suppose you went to the employees in your organization and asked, "What is the number-one objective of our company?" How many different answers do you think you would get? Would management answer the question the same way that the front-line employees would? In the 1991 movie *City Slickers,* the lead character (played by Billy Crystal) is a middle-aged man who goes out West to find himself. He is having a midlife crisis and is looking for meaning in his life. He runs into a grizzled old cowboy (played by Jack Palance) who is very straightforward and asks him, "Do you know what the secret of life is?" When the Crystal character doesn't respond, the cowboy holds up his index finger and says, "One thing . . . just one thing: You focus on that and nothing else means (anything)." Crystal says, "Great, but what is the one thing?" And the cowboy responds, "That is what *you* have to figure out."

Companies are the same way. It is extremely important that everyone in the organization be focused on the same overall goal. The strategy map provides the perfect format to illustrate what that goal is. It is typically listed at the top of the map, and several arrows are drawn into it. The arrows originate at supporting objectives that the company deems necessary to achieving the overall number one. Consider the example from a state Treasury in Exhibit 4.1.

EXHIBIT 4.1 *Department of the Treasury Strategy Map*

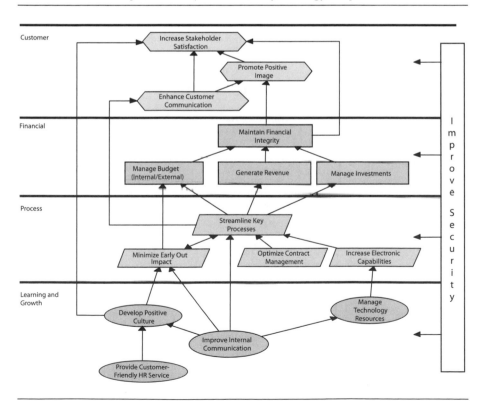

Note the number one objective, titled *Increase Stakeholder Satisfaction,* is listed at the top of the map. Stakeholders in the organization included the state individual and business taxpayers, the recipients of the educational grants administered by the Treasury, the governor, and the legislature; the organization was responsible for satisfying a diverse group of external parties. Note that four arrows lead directly into *Increase Stakeholder Satisfaction.* These should be read as an IF-THEN statement. In this case, IF the organization *Promotes a Positive Image, Enhances Customer Communication, Maintains Financial Integrity,* and *Develops a Positive Culture,* THEN it will *Increase Stakeholder Satisfaction.* In other words, the supporting objectives illustrate what is necessary from a cause-and-effect perspective to make the top objective happen. These relationships hold throughout the diagram. The Finance section provides another excellent example: IF the organization *Manages Budget, Generates Revenue,* and *Manages Investments,* THEN it will *Maintain Financial Integrity.* Note that this particular diagram has a great deal of focus on *Streamlining Internal Processes.* The reason for this is that the Treasury was in the midst of its second early retirement program within the last five years. The impact was loss of over 30% of its employee base, most of whom had the longest tenure with the organization. Since this reduction did not come with a corresponding reduction of responsibilities, it was imperative to improve process efficiency. To that end, *Increasing Electronic Capabilities* would raise the percentage of taxpayers who could file electronically, reducing the pressure to process manual returns. *Optimizing Contract Management* would enable outsourcing of certain functions, reducing pressure on internal resources. Because they were allowed to select replacements for those accepting the early retirement on a 1-to-4 or 1-to-5 basis, *Minimizing Early Out Impact* directed them to select which positions needed to be filled the most from a strategic perspective to keep their key processes functioning properly.

Connecting objectives in this way forces the leadership team to think cross-functionally. It takes them out of the component strategy mindset and forces them to think holistically. One of the more productive meetings in the entire strategic process is the one in which the leadership team sits down to discuss and debate the connections. It often happens that a preselected objective cannot be connected to the remaining objectives. There are two possibilities when this occurs: One is that the lone objective is really not connected to anything else, in which case the organization should question whether it should be an ongoing part of the strategy. The other possibility is yet-to-be-determined objectives would help connect the lone objective to everything else, and the assessment process did not identify them. In this case the management team should identify and add whatever needs to be added to complete the picture. It follows that one of the more valuable uses for the strategy map is to ensure that an integrated set of objectives emerges.

Note the categories, or *perspectives*, listed in the upper left-hand corner of each layer of the map. In this case, the four perspectives are Financial, Customer, Process, and Learning and Growth. These follow the flow of the strategic assessment process described in the prior chapter. The hierarchy for each individual company is determined by the cause-and-effect relationship among the perspectives. In a for-profit organization, the hierarchy is usually simple to establish and is illustrated in Exhibit 4.2.

Starting at the bottom, Learning and Growth consists of those things that fuel strong Process performance. Developing people, promoting strong internal communication, building good systems, and so on are things that companies of today must do to drive process success. At the next level, the strategy map targets the processes that are key to the future of the organization and establishes objectives for them as well. These processes are typically the ones customers care most about, or the things the company must be proficient in to keep their customers happy. And the resulting customer satisfaction in turn drives financial results. There usually isn't much discussion to be had when establishing these relationships.

Not-for-profit organizations are a bit different. The strategy map is marginally tougher to construct because the position of the Financial section isn't as obvious. Some organizations, like the Memorial Blood Center of Minneapolis, retain the traditional hierarchy with Financial at the top. One of its critical issues is recruiting enough donors to keep the blood

EXHIBIT 4.2   *Relationship of Strategy Map Perspectives:*
For-Profit Organization

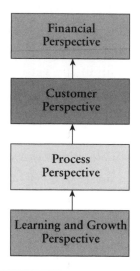

supply sufficient to area hospitals. The service fees generated by this activity help the organization *Maintain Acceptable Operating Margins*, which was the top objective on its first strategy map. The organization reasoned that it needed the financial focus on top because the ultimate outcome was to stay in business so "that others might live," as inscribed on their cornerstone plaque. And they couldn't stay in business without acceptable operating margin.

Other not-for-profit organizations view the Financial section a bit differently. The Treasury example in Exhibit 4.1, for instance, has Financial positioned as shown in Exhibit 4.3.

The thinking in this instance is that the ultimate goal of the not-for-profit is to satisfy customers, and one component of this is sound financial management. In other words, taxpayers want the Treasury to be cost efficient and provide service at minimal fees. This explains not only why Financial is important to customer satisfaction, but also why Process efficiency is linked to financial performance. Learning and Growth support

EXHIBIT **4.3** *Relationship of Strategy Map Perspectives:*
Not-for-Profit Organization

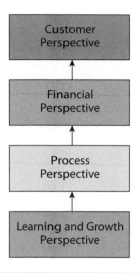

Process performance as in the for-profit model. This hierarchy is probably the most common in a not-for-profit sense.

A third way to view Financial is to place it at the very bottom of the chain, as shown in Exhibit 4.4. This is the format utilized by the Michigan State University Vet School when developing its strategy map.

The vet school reasoned that its entire strategy was fueled by tuition dollars, and once these were generated, it would have the money to fund learning and growth initiatives, which in turn would lead to good process performance and ultimately result in customer satisfaction.

So which flow of perspectives is correct? All of them. The secret for the not-for-profit company is to select the format that tells the story the way the organization wishes to tell it; there isn't an answer that is universally correct. This concept also extends to the names of the perspectives. While most strategy maps follow the traditional four-perspective format, there is nothing magical about the four traditional categories. If a fifth perspective is needed, or if the company wishes to rename one of the four to

EXHIBIT 4.4   *Relationship of Strategy Map Perspectives:*
               Not-for-Profit Organization Alternative

better reflect its business situation, then so be it. The process to be covered
for strategy map development has some flexibility built in to identify
when additional or different perspectives might be necessary.

Examples of additional perspectives used by different organizations
in the past include environmental, health and safety, product, and supplier; the list of potential candidates is long. The key is that the organization considers a particular category to be of such strategic importance
that it needs to be elevated to perspective level. Going back to the Treasury example, notice the bar down the right-hand side of the diagram labeled *Improve Security*. When developing their strategy map, the team
realized that they managed a huge financial portfolio (i.e., all of the
state's tax money) and had access to a great deal of confidential information (i.e., all residents' personal financial data). It was determined
that if they didn't have strong security of dollars and data, everything
else was irrelevant. Hence, security was elevated to perspective level
and placed along the side of the map, with general arrows flowing into
each perspective symbolizing that security drove everything.

An excellent example of a for-profit strategy map comes from the Orion Development Group. As noted in the prior chapter during the customer segmentation example, Orion specializes in strategic planning and process improvement. The first strategy map developed by the organization is provided in Exhibit 4.5.

There are several interesting points to be made about this strategy map. The number-one objective is *Maintain Strong Financial Position*. While this is not remarkable, note that the only objective feeding into the top is *Increase Revenue*. A reader unfamiliar with the organization would (correctly) suppose that there is a missing financial objective here; it would seem that in this case the IF-THEN statement would be incomplete. In other words, to say "IF we *Increase Revenue,* THEN we will *Maintain a Strong Financial Position"* excludes the cost side of the equation. While

EXHIBIT 4.5   *Consulting Company Strategy Map*

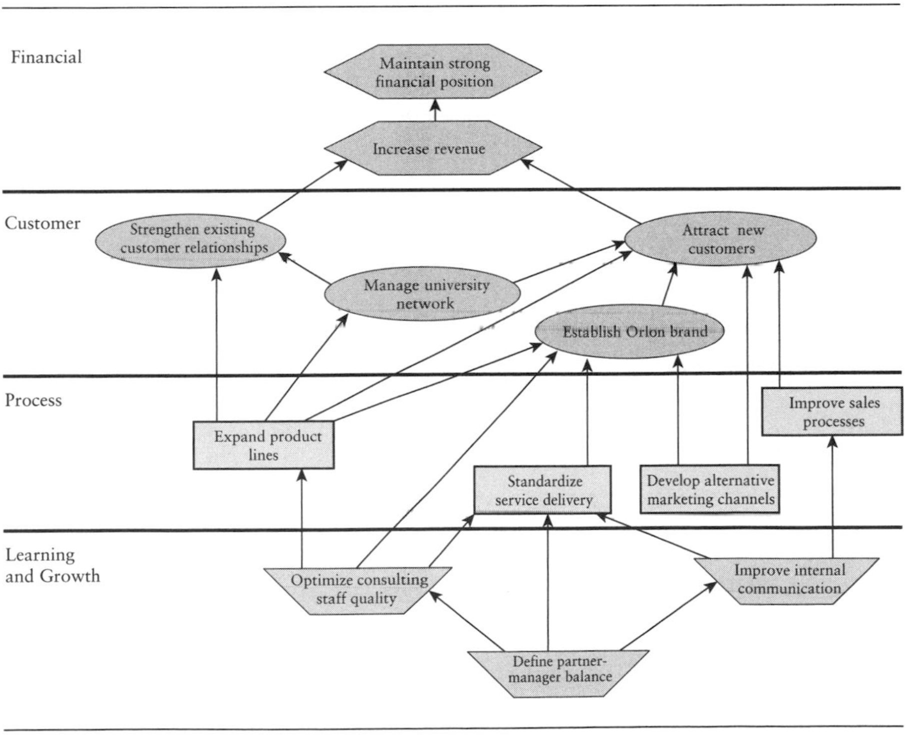

this is true, Orion has a somewhat unique business model. The vast majority of the company expenses are paid to consultants who have been trained to deliver their materials. These consultants are not salaried employees; they are paid on a per diem or per project basis structured around how much work they actually do. So if they aren't working, Orion isn't paying. This means that the company is not under pressure (like most of its competitors are) to sell services just to make payroll. Because most of their staff has separate consulting practices to draw business from, Orion can focus on taking only those engagements that are mutually beneficial to itself and its clients. So, since cost is proportional to revenue, increasing revenue is enough to help the company *Maintain a Strong Financial Position.*

Dropping down into the customer perspective, note that there are two objectives entitled *Strengthen Existing Customer Relationships* and *Attract New Customers.* These both sound very generic and could appear on virtually any organization's strategy map. Very few Boards of Directors would look at objectives like these and exclaim, "Great job, leadership team! Who would have ever thought that attracting new customers was something we should focus on!" There are two important topics to consider when titling objectives. Some leaders of the strategy mapping methodology would say that the customer objectives should reflect value propositions offered to the customer. For example, instead of *Attract New Customers*, the objective might be retitled to say *Provide Differentiated Product/Service Combinations to New Customers.* This could provide insights into what the company thinks will attract the new customers; namely, the product line expansion referenced in the Process section.

If your organization feels that the objectives sound better by adding more detail, then you should do it that way. But however it is done, remember that the process to be described for building the map utilizes all the data gathered during the strategic assessment phase. The objective titled *Attract New Customers* might be consistent from company to company, but all the issues relating to it will differ dramatically. This means that when it is time to select measures and initiatives for successful new customer attraction, the choices will be based on the data gathered during their own unique assessment. For this reason, some companies decide to keep the top-level map as simple as possible and let the uniqueness emerge in the more detailed planning levels.

Note the volume of arrows flowing in to *Attract New Customers*. While it is unwise to simply count the number of arrows and assume that this establishes the hierarchy of importance, in this case it certainly appears that finding new customers is a main focus area for the organization. Because the cost structure previously referenced virtually guarantees that new customers mean more profitability, it makes sense that attraction would be of paramount importance.

One of the more significant objectives on the map is *Establish Orion Brand*. Note that the objectives leading into this are *Expand Product Lines, Standardize Service Delivery, Develop Alternative Marketing Channels*, and *Optimize Consulting Staff Quality*. The message given here is that the organization wants to establish that the combination of its people, products, and methodology make it unique.

The Learning and Growth objectives also make important statements. Almost every organization could *Improve Internal Communication*, but in Orion's case it is particularly critical. The consultants are the service providers. Not only are they scattered throughout the country, but most of them aren't even full-time Orion employees. Ensuring that all service providers are on the same page and up to speed with curriculum updates and project requirements is a monster challenge. But if the objective of *Standardizing Service Delivery* is to be met, Orion must find ways to overcome the communication barriers. Nothing leads to dissatisfied customers and lost business faster than multiple consultants telling a client different things. The communication objective also feeds *Improve Sales Processes*. The consulting staff has expertise in a wide variety of industries and methodologies. When a new sales opportunity comes along, it obviously increases the probability of closing the deal if Orion can reference its experience in relevant areas. The problem at the time was that there was no central database to keep track of such things, leading to less convincing proposals and potentially lost business.

The objective at the bottom of the map is *Define Partner/Manager Balance*. This is the foundation of the map, meaning that focus on this would be necessary to fuel everything else. The reason this objective is so critical is that Orion has no formal management team. In other words, there isn't a group of people paid to manage everything or everyone else. The partners in the organization are also their service line practice leaders. Sometimes the tendency of the partners is to get so wrapped up in service delivery that they neglect overall management responsibilities. This behavior is reinforced by the fact that service delivery is more directly connected to revenue generation than are management responsibilities. So the organization felt conscious effort was needed to ensure that future growth was being planned for as well as today's bottom-line performance.

The use of strategy maps does not have to be confined to the organization-wide level. An excellent example of a functional area strategy map comes from the Human Resources Department at Texas Children's Hospital (TCH). The organization is in an extremely aggressive growth phase, expanding from 3,000 to an eventual 7,000 employees over the span of a few short years. The HR department recognized the tremendous challenges they would face in supporting the organization in the face of such aggressive growth, and their planning session yielded the strategy map shown in Exhibit 4.6.

The first instructive point is the hierarchy of objectives. Since HR is a support function, it is only natural for Customer to go on top, but note that in this case Customer refers to internal versus external parties. For HR to be deemed ultimately successful, the operating areas of the hospital must receive the service they need, and the executive team must be convinced that the service provided by HR is being delivered in a cost-effective and efficient manner. So the Customer perspective is at the top, driven heavily by the Financial and Process perspectives. Learning and Growth occupies its familiar position at the base, providing the foundation for strong performance.

The HR department at TCH is very progressive in their thinking. Continuous Quality Improvement (CQI) was initiated at the hospital in the early 1990s and still flourishes more than a dozen years later. The HR management team has internalized the concepts to the point that

EXHIBIT 4.6   *Texas Children's Hospital Human Resource Department Strategy Map*

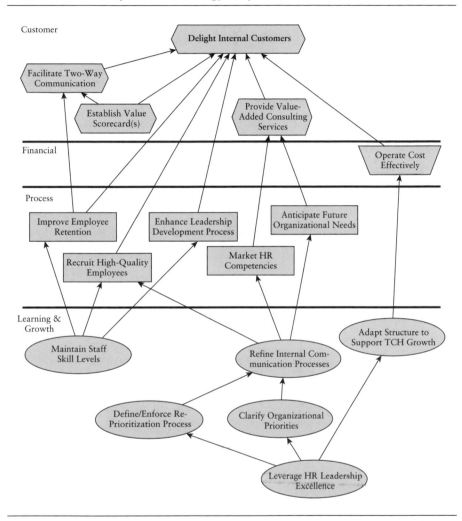

problem solving and process improvement is truly a way of life for them. This made the strategy mapping session extremely interesting, and resulted in a map containing objectives that one wouldn't traditionally look for on a Human Resources planning document.

For example, note that in the Customer section there are objectives of *Establish Value Scorecards* and *Provide Value-Added Consulting*

Services. Obviously, if the department was delivering value-added services, it would make its internal customers happy—if they recognized it. The idea behind the value scorecards was to be able to demonstrate to the operating areas that HR was providing this quality service that literally added value. The purpose was *not* to make HR look good; it was to illustrate how the department could assist operating areas in making their jobs easier. It was felt that demonstration of value would lead to increased reliance on HR to execute the necessary personnel-related processes, freeing up the clinical areas to focus on what they wanted to focus on: treating sick children. This would certainly help achieve the top objective of *Delighting Internal Customers.*

Another instructive point can be made from the Process perspective. Note that some of the objectives are to *Recruit High-Quality Employees, Improve Employee Retention,* and *Enhance the Leadership Development Process.* If this were an organization-wide strategy map, these would all be housed in the Learning and Growth perspective. All of them deal with support processes that from the top level would be viewed as fueling core process performance. In the case of HR, however, processes like recruiting, retention, and leadership development *are* core processes; those are the things HR is set up to do. So their presence in the Process section is completely appropriate. And obviously recruiting and retention are both definitely worthy of objective-level importance, given that the organization was trying to more than double its employee base in a relatively short time span. Leadership development would be instrumental in preventing chaos in the midst of all the growth.

Note that in the Learning and Growth section there is an objective of *Maintain Staff Skill Levels.* This refers to the internal HR staff. In the process to be covered for development of the strategy map, the choice of verb will be referenced as an important issue. To say *maintain* in this sense implies that the skill level of current HR employees is excellent, or at least good enough that the management team doesn't feel it needs to be improved upon. And in the case of human resources at TCH, this was certainly the case. This reinforces the base objective of the entire map, which was to *Leverage HR Leadership Excellence.*

The strategy map has grown in popularity over the years. The tool was part of the original Balanced Scorecard methodology introduced by Kaplan and Norton in the early 1990s. But for whatever reason, many organizations failed to incorporate the map into their strategic process right away. Many organizations heard "scorecard" and immediately latched on to the measurement aspects of the process. Even today many organizations that have been focused on Balanced Scorecards for years are discovering that the strategy map can help them fill gaps in their strategic process. It is critically important for development and communication of strategy.

STRATEGY MAP: IMPLEMENTATION

The process for developing the strategy map involves taking all the data gathered through the (formal or informal) strategic assessment process and using it to determine what the objectives should be—and then linking them together. The process will be separated into two phases: objective identification and linkage. The formal process for objective identification is illustrated in Exhibit 4.7.

The assessment process was utilized to identify the strategic issues (strengths, weaknesses, opportunities, and threats) that impact the organization's ability to achieve the parameters established in its mission

EXHIBIT **4.7** *Strategy Map Development Process: Objective Identification*

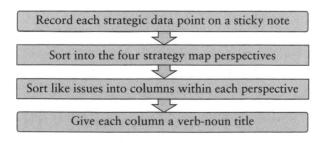

and vision. It is not uncommon to have more than 200 issues identified through the various tools and techniques. This can be overwhelming without a good process for focusing and refining, so following the steps illustrated in Exhibit 4.7 is crucial.

Begin by recording each strategic issue on its own individual sticky note. Establish five areas in the room, labeled:

1. Financial
2. Customer
3. Process
4. Learning and Growth
5. ???

All of the sticky notes should be lined up under the "???" category to begin with. The leadership team responsible for the development of the strategy should then go to the sticky notes and start pulling them off the "???" area and placing them in the category that each one is most closely associated with. Some ground rules and tips to assist in the placement are as follows.

Use "Cheat Sheets"

To assist in placement, put a reference note beside each perspective category that gives insights into what types of things should be sorted there. For example, the reference for Learning and Growth could be:

- People
- Internal Communication
- Support Stuff

It should be explained that People refers to *your* people, not customers. Hiring them, training them, keeping them, keeping them happy, and so on. And Internal Communication refers to your people talking to your people, not to customers or the external world. Support Stuff is what your organization does to keep the wheels turning, but that really isn't a part of the core business. If you are an insurance company, for example, it is critical to have a good disaster recovery plan to prevent you from losing critical data on losses, customers, and so forth. But an insurance company is not in the disaster recovery business (except for paying for other companies' disasters!), so this would be a Support Stuff issue.

The cheat sheet for the Process section should include core internal process issues as well as product and service delivery issues. The Customer category in for-profit companies could include external customers, the community, industry, market, brand image, reputation—anything representing the external view. This is not meant to be an exhaustive list, because some things are industry-dependent. For example, an insurance company would list its broker network in the Customer section as well. Financial is pretty straightforward—it's all about the money.

These cheat sheets are useful because they help speed up the organization of what could be a very large quantity of information. The best technique is to place the tips on sticky notes next to the perspective titles and then remove them once all the notes are sorted. (The reason for removing them is to prevent predetermined categories for the next round of sorting, which will be explained shortly.)

Sort by the Fact, Not by the Implications of the Fact

Recall that the process for recording S.W.O.T.s emphasized that each issue include both fact and implications. The proper technique for sorting is to focus on the fact as the categorization criteria. For example, consider the comment:

> Well-trained employees help build strong long-term customer relationships.

This would be placed in the Learning and Growth category, since the fact is well-trained employees. The long-term customer relationships would be the outcome of this, so it wouldn't be placed in the Customer section. Similarly, the suggestion:

Bringing new products to market takes too long, causing us to lose our competitive edge.

would probably be viewed as a process issue, if the fact was related to the product development process. Losing the competitive edge would be the customer-related outcome.

It is natural to question why so much emphasis is placed on including the implications of the fact as part of the S.W.O.T. if it is ignored during the sorting phase. The answer will be evident when drawing the connections between the objectives when building the strategy map. For example, an objective of *Developing Employee Skills* might be instrumental for streamlining processes in one organization and equally vital for building customer relationships in another. The implications of the fact aid in the determination of desired outcomes in each case.

Don't Force the Sticky Notes into a Particular Column

Recall that every strategy map does not necessarily have to fit into the four standard objectives. It is entirely possible that, when analyzing the sticky notes in the "???" category, the group will feel that some of the issues don't really fit into any of the perspectives. When this happens, the group should leave them in the "???" category until sorting is complete. At this juncture, the group should analyze all of the issues that weren't sorted and determine if there is some connection between them. If this is the case, the next step is to determine whether the overall topic is important enough to be elevated to perspective level. If so, then a fifth perspective may be born and added to the model.

Keep Talking to a Minimum

This is the easiest ground rule to understand but sometimes the hardest one to follow. The first sort should not take very long, probably 10 to 15 minutes at most. If the participants start getting into long-winded discussions about the positioning of each sticky note, then this could take far longer than necessary. A useful facilitation technique is to remind participants that the notes are not fastened to the initial area with super glue. In other words, if you discover later in the process that they are better suited in another category, you can always move them. The purpose of this first sort is simply to start putting some structure to the massive amount of assessment data; it is not to place every note 100% perfectly.

Don't Try to Balance the Notes Across the Perspectives

In other words, don't feel like there should be 25% of the notes in the Financial category, 25% in the Customer category, and so on. In fact, it would be very surprising if it turned out this way. Generally speaking, the closer to the bottom of the strategy map hierarchy you get, the more sticky notes will reside. So Learning and Growth will almost always have the most notes (in either for-profit or not-for-profit organizations), Process will be a close second, and the least will be in the Customer and Financial categories.

This does not imply that Financial is the least important or that there were gaps in the assessment process. Rather, it is a reflection of the rule to sort by fact versus implications of the fact. A quick review of the sticky notes will usually reveal that almost all of the issues will have either customer or financial *implications*, but the *facts* on the notes will be of a process or people nature. Because of this, it isn't unusual to have a sparse Financial section. This typically is not a problem, however. The purpose of this process is to ultimately determine a good set of strategic objectives, and most organizations are extremely proficient at developing financial objectives to fill any gaps that might be present.

The next step in the objective development process is to sort similar issues into columns within each perspective. In other words, the group should begin with the Learning and Growth perspective. Look at all of the sticky notes present in the category and look for common themes. The group should start pulling the notes off the wall (or whatever they are sticking to) and realign them into columns that are connected somehow. In other words, the objective is to go from what is shown in Exhibit 4.8 to what is shown in Exhibit 4.9.

EXHIBIT **4.8**　*Learning and Growth S.W.O.T.s: Unsorted*

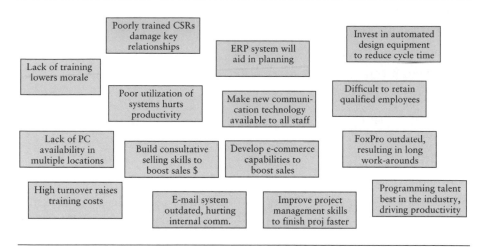

EXHIBIT **4.9**　*Learning and Growth S.W.O.T.s: Sorted*

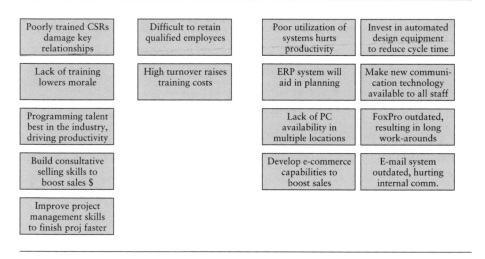

Column one appears to be related to training and skill development, column two about employee retention, and column three deals with support technology issues. While this might seem straightforward with an example that lists only 15 issues, it can get very difficult when starting with over 200. Tips to make the sorting process easier are as follows:

- *Think global:* The group should shoot for three or four columns *maximum*. The columns will eventually be titled and used for objectives on the strategy map, so it isn't advisable to have too many of them. It will dilute the focus on all objectives and unnecessarily clutter the map. Therefore, instructing the group to shoot for three or four is the best way to proceed. If they wind up with five, then it really isn't a problem, but they shouldn't wind up with fifteen!

- *Don't sort into S.W.O.T. categories:* In other words, instruct the group that the connections they see should *not* be strengths, weaknesses, opportunities, or threats. If one sticky note references "excellent training" and another references "poor training" and the group puts them in the same column that is training-based, that would be fine. But there shouldn't be a "good stuff" column and a "bad stuff" column. The reason for this will soon become evident. The next step is to title the columns, and these titles will serve as the objectives for the strategy map. Sorting into the S.W.O.T. categories would yield strategic objectives of *Maximize Strengths, Minimize Weaknesses,* and so forth. Because these would not really be meaningful, stick with the content of the fact on the sticky note versus whether it reflects a particular S.W.O.T. category.

  The most common mistake made when applying this rule is in the Customer category. External issues that deal with competitors and the marketplace typically get grouped into a category together, and when the time comes to title the column, the line of reasoning in grouping them is often, "Well, these are the things that we can't do anything about." This often is simply a disguised threats column. The facilitator should be on guard for this issue and direct the group to look for other connections beyond the fact that the issues are negative external influences and possibilities.

- *Don't split into subgroups:* The common sense method for executing this sort is to divide and conquer. In other words, if the leadership team consists of 12 executives and there are four perspectives, it seems natural to put three members into each perspective and sort all four groups simultaneously. This is one time in which intuition can lead a group astray, however. Because the high-level sort was done with massive amounts of data, it is only natural that there will be sticky notes that are not categorized properly (*properly* in this case means categorized with all others of its kind, with no mismatched notes). Because of this, simultaneous sorting will generally yield one or two columns in each perspective that are very logical, and the remaining notes will form a potpourri of issues that is difficult to categorize. Because notes in the potpourri from one perspective will be scattered with the potpourri in other perspectives, it typically takes quite a while to straighten everything out. So long, in fact, that doing the sorting as a full group and moving from perspective to perspective is typically the superior approach.

So the recommendation is to have the entire group begin with the Learning and Growth perspective. Even though this is where the highest volume of notes is usually located, the categories are typically the easiest to identify. If any notes do not immediately appear to fit into the established columns, question whether they should perhaps be relocated to one of the other perspectives. When the sorting has been completed, the group may either

- ○ Title the columns following the guidelines in the next step, or
- ○ Move along to the next perspective and repeat the sorting process, and then title all of the objectives at the end of the sorting.

- *Keep talking to a minimum:* This is even more important now than it was in the last step. Analyzing the sticky notes and finding common themes should be done silently. If the group is not allowed to talk, then everyone will have an equal say. In other words, the one or two dominant personalities in the group will not be able to control everything. If this is allowed to happen, the process will not only take much longer, but the resulting product will typically not be as good. Talking fosters the practice of naming the columns too quickly and then trying to force the rest of the notes into the predetermined categories. It is far better to stay silent and try to understand the reasoning of the other team members as the sticky notes are lined up. The group members should feel free to move the sticky notes to other columns if they aren't comfortable with the placement, but they can't talk about it.

Each of the perspectives will present unique challenges when attempting to sort the issues. The challenge in the Learning and Growth section is dealing with the sheer volume of information. The challenge in the Financial section is just the opposite: coming up with the right set of objectives using what is certain to be a limited number of sticky notes. The Customer section will be difficult due to the aforementioned tendency to establish a threats column. But the most difficult section to perfect is typically the Process section.

This is an especially important point because the focus of the first few chapters was about how Process is becoming more and more of a force in driving strategy. So why is the Process perspective the hardest one to nail down? One reason is the aforementioned fact that there are literally thousands of processes in a typical organization. Trying to determine which few have strategic significance can be a daunting task. The group should look for connections in the sticky notes that reference specific processes, while still trying to keep a manageable number of columns. This is never an easy task.

Referring back to the Process section of the Treasury strategy map, there was an objective of *Streamline Key Processes*. This is not an ideal title, as it is very general and doesn't reference specific processes, but in the case of Treasury it was justified. Their organization was very diverse, consisting of a tax branch, an education branch, a local government branch, and several authorities. The decision they made was to have an overall objective of streamlining key processes, and when time came for plan execution and measurement, they would select one from each area to improve. (For this reason, it was important to insert the word *key* into the objective. Without it, the implication is that the company is initiating a broad campaign to streamline *all* processes.) Generally speaking, however, it is wise to avoid such a general title if possible. Treasury was simply trying to avoid having too many titles for objectives, which is laudable. But many organizations are just post-poning the decision of which processes need attention and focus by having such a general title to begin with. (In other words, when the time comes to establish measures for an objective of *Streamline Key Processes*, the group will *then* have to decide which processes are the key ones before they determine appropriate measures, and the same holds true for the establishment of process improvement initiatives.)

The final step in the objective development process is to give each column a verb-noun title. In other words, put each title in the form of "do something-to something." This will produce action-oriented objectives that fit together logically on the strategy map. The ground rules for this step are as follows:

- *Pick the verb that best characterizes your intended action:* Incorrect choice of a verb will obviously not doom the company, but the choice should reflect the action you intend to take. For example, the TCH Human Resources strategy map had the objective of *Maintain Staff Skill Levels.* This obviously sends the message that the level is strong already, and what is needed is simply to keep it where it is. If the wording was *Enhance Staff Skill Levels,* then the message sent is a little different. This implies that while the skill level might not be atrocious, there is still room for improvement. A title of *Upgrade Staff Skill Levels* sends another different message: that the current levels are clearly insufficient to support the execution of the strategy, so new skills are needed. Again, pick the verb that best summarizes your intended action.

- *Don't overuse the same verb:* This might sound like a ridiculous rule, but the tendency when naming objectives for the first time is to use the same two or three verbs over and over (*improve* and *develop* are the most common choices). While there is nothing technically wrong with reusing the same verb, it causes the map to lose credibility. Consider the following IF-THEN statement: IF we *Improve Staff Skills* and *Improve Internal Communication* and

Improve Outsourcing, THEN we will *Improve Internal Processes*. While this might certainly be true, it sounds so obvious that it won't be taken seriously. It sounds like no thought has been given to the objectives. Since one of the purposes of building a strategy map is to have a vehicle to communicate strategy, it is imperative not to have a map that is rejected on sight because it doesn't look like sufficient thought was put into developing it.

Try to put a one-objective maximum on the use of each verb. If you feel you need to use one twice, it isn't a problem, but be as diverse as possible while still conveying the proper intent for each objective.

- *Remember that politics count:* Suppose that during the assessment phase several S.W.O.Ts were identified that hinted at deficiencies within the management team (e.g., lack of vision, lack of cooperation, silo thinking). These issues were grouped together in a column in the Learning and Growth perspective, and now the management team has the assignment of giving the column a title. A title like *Upgrade Management Capabilities* might accurately summarize the issues on the list, but there isn't likely to be much support for an objective with such a title, and think of the fiasco when presenting such an objective to the board or the workforce—probably not the image the company wants to create.

  There are two alternatives the company could pursue in a case like this. The first is to reason that the management team is part of the workforce, and if there is another column filled with workforce development issues, these could all be grouped together. If this is the course the company decided to pursue, it would be imperative to select initiatives to execute that would aid in management development.

  The other possibility is to rename the objective in a more positive fashion. If the management team felt the issues in the column were real and didn't want to "sweep them under the rug" by combining them with employee development issues, then a title such as *Formalize Management Development Program* might be an option.

Think about your organization: When someone is promoted to management, how is that person typically trained? Many organizations have no preparatory programs for new managers at all. But for argument's sake, assume your organization does have a program for employees when they first get promoted into the management ranks. What happens the next time they take a step up the corporate ladder? And the time after that? And the time after that? Many times organizations promote the accounts payable clerk to finance manager to controller to CFO to COO to CEO, never giving him or her training in how to manage increasingly diverse areas. If this is the case in your organization, an objective title such as *Formalize Management Development Program* would convey the message that management skills need further refinement, but puts the responsibility for creating the gap on the process versus the individual. This is much more likely to get acceptance and buy-in both inside and outside of the management team.

The major point to be made is that if the objective titles are offensive to the parties responsible for the execution of strategy, then it is highly unlikely that strategy will be executed. So the goal is not to ignore problems, but to illustrate them in such a way as to give the highest probability they can be addressed effectively.

Note that the objective-setting process will involve some trial and error. There is no magic answer to what topics are worthy of being perspectives or objectives. There is not a perfect number of objectives. A good facilitation question when trying to determine if a particular topic is worthy of being an objective is, "If we only had three objectives in this perspective, would the column in question be important enough to rank as one of the top three?" For example, consider the Learning and Growth objective of *Improve Internal Communication*. Communication is so poor in some organizations that it would definitely merit consideration as one of the top three objectives. Poor communication could cause inefficient process performance, decreased customer satisfaction, and lost revenue. In other organizations, poor communication might be a minor irritation—nice to fix but not really that significant.

The good news is that the learning curve on objective development is very steep when using this process. After going through it once or twice, the facilitator (and team members) will quickly get much better at it. The process has been used in many organizations over the last several years, and it is a telling statement that the vast majority of organizations have stuck with it after becoming familiar with it. A vice president of a major insurance company remarked that, "I've been doing strategic planning for thirty years, and I've never seen a process that cuts through the nonsense as fast as this one does." Indeed, the sorting and titling process should take less than a day if the S.WO.T.s have been identified prior to the meeting, which can be a dramatic reduction in time over other objective-setting methods.

Once the objectives have been identified, it is time to move to the linkage segment of strategy map development. Assume the set of objectives illustrated in Exhibit 4.10 were determined during the objective identification phase. These will be used throughout the explanation of the linkage exercise to assist in the understanding of strategy map development.

The steps for linkage are illustrated in Exhibit 4.11.

The first step is to determine the number-one objective of the organization. This will be the objective that draws the most attention, as it will sit at the top of the strategy map. The process flowchart also includes the selection of the number-one perspective, which obviously would need to happen before the objective is selected. In most cases, the top perspective will be obvious, but there are exceptions. For example, if you were developing a functional strategy map for the claims department of an insurance company, what would your top perspective and objective be? Finance isn't a clear-cut choice, because this would reinforce the behavior of denying claims that perhaps shouldn't be denied. Customer satisfaction isn't a clear-cut choice either, because it could reinforce the behavior of paying claims that shouldn't be paid. So the claims organization would be in a quandary regarding which perspective

EXHIBIT 4.10   *Strategy Map Objectives: Demo*

Perspective	Objectives		
Financial	Maximize profitability	Reduce costs	
Customer	Penetrate new markets	Maintain top reputation	Build strong relationships
Process	Optimize supply chain	Increase on time delivery	Accelerate product development time
Learning & Growth	Develop high quality staff	Upgrade systems	Improve internal communication

EXHIBIT 4.11   *Strategy Map Development: Linkage Process*

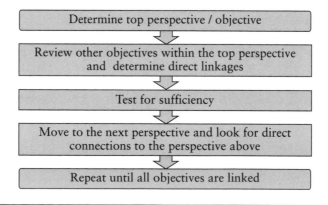

Determine top perspective / objective

Review other objectives within the top perspective and determine direct linkages

Test for sufficiency

Move to the next perspective and look for direct connections to the perspective above

Repeat until all objectives are linked

should be placed on top. Thankfully, however, this is a rare case. In a general sense, for-profit organizations will start with Financial, and not-for-profit organizations will start with Customer. Functional strategy maps will almost always start with Customer on the top as well, although the customers referenced will often be internal.

The proper technique for performing the first step of the flowchart is to review the objectives in the top perspective that were previously named. The idea is to determine whether any of the identified categories is suitable to serve as the number-one objective for the organization. For the purposes of this demonstration, there are two Financial objectives, with titles of *Maximize Profitability* and *Reduce Costs*. Of the two choices, *Maximize Profitability* is really the only option for a top objective. Costs are important, but the company focused only on costs will have difficulty being successful over the long term. There is an old business axiom that states that you cannot shrink to greatness, so a singular focus on cost reduction is typically not the most productive strategy.

Note: From a not-for-profit perspective, it is important to choose a top Customer objective. The Treasury example yielded a top objective of *Maximize Stakeholder Satisfaction,* which is certainly an acceptable number-one goal. Other not-for-profits have gotten more creative with their top spot. The Delaware River Port Authority (DRPA), for example, adopted *Keep the Region Moving* as its top objective. This was actually the mission statement of the organization, so it fit nicely at the summit. The statement had a double meaning: DRPA was responsible for managing the trains, bridges, ferry, cruises, and so on in the area, so keeping the region moving had a transportation facet to it. But the organization was also responsible for attracting tourists to the Camden-Philadelphia area waterfront, so keeping the region moving also had an economic angle to it.

Another interesting example is the Parks and Recreation Department of a major county government. The first choice for top objective was *Provide Continuous Service.* While there is nothing technically wrong with this objective, it really isn't very inspiring. When questioned on the meaning of *Provide Continuous Service*, team members commented that they would like to give the citizens of the county recreation options 24/7. In light of this, the top objective was changed to a more thought-provoking *Play All Day*. While the change was primarily cosmetic, it did help the department tell a more interesting story when explaining its strategy to stakeholders.

The next step of the process is to determine which other objectives within the top perspective directly cause the number-one objective to happen. And *direct* means that a simple IF-THEN statement can be made that logically ties the two objectives together. In the previous example, it could easily be understood that IF the organization *Reduces Costs*, THEN it would be more likely to *Maximize Profitability*. As is the case throughout the mapping process, if there are objectives within this perspective that do not seem to fit, consider adding additional objectives to make the connections more clear, or drop the objective in isolation.

The third step says that the group should test for sufficiency. This means that in the previous step it was established that *Reducing Costs* is *necessary* to help *Maximize Profitability*, but now is the time to question whether cost reduction would be enough by itself. Clearly, in this case it would not, as the generation of additional revenue would be instrumental in the maximization of profit. If this were in fact determined to be the case, it is appropriate to add another objective related to revenue generation. So the completed Financial perspective of the strategy map would be as shown in Exhibit 4.12.

EXHIBIT 4.12   *Demo Strategy Map: Financial Perspective*

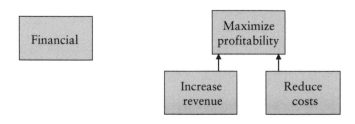

Once the top section is complete, the next step is to move to the next perspective. In a for-profit organization this would be the Customer section. The proper question to ask is, "Which Customer objectives directly cause one of the Financial objectives to happen?" Look for the most direct link between any of the Customer objectives and any single Financial objective, and draw the connecting arrow into it. The Customer objectives that are candidates for demonstration purposes are *Maintain Top Reputation, Penetrate New Markets,* and *Build Strong Customer Relationships*. When looking for connections between these and the objectives in the Financial section, it appears that direct links would occur between *Increase Revenue* and both *Penetrate New Markets* and *Build Strong Customer Relationships*. In fact, this relationship makes a great deal of sense, as it implies that keeping current customers and finding new ones are instrumental for revenue growth. The organization must then decide how to position the *Maintain Top Reputation* objective. Because the title includes the verb *maintain*, it is clear that the reputation is already strong. It is reasonable to assume that the reputation would be leveraged to help *Penetrate New Markets*.

Depending on the industry, it might be reasonable to assume reputation would drive *Build Strong Customer Relationships* as well. For example, an investment banking firm like Goldman Sachs has an excellent reputation, and customers might remain with the organization because there is prestige in simply being a client. On the other hand, a retail company such as Wal-Mart also has an excellent reputation, but customers searching for low prices might abandon the chain for another store if better prices became available. Pursuing the first option would yield a strategy map linking the objectives in the top two perspectives, as shown in Exhibit 4.13.

Note that there are no customer objectives feeding the *Reduce Costs* objective. It is not uncommon to bypass the cost side when evaluating objectives within the Customer perspective. In other words, many times all of the objectives in the Customer section feed up through the revenue side straight to the overall top objective. Some inexperienced facilitators get nervous about this phenomenon and try to invent connections between

EXHIBIT 4.13 *Demo Strategy Map: Customer Perspective*

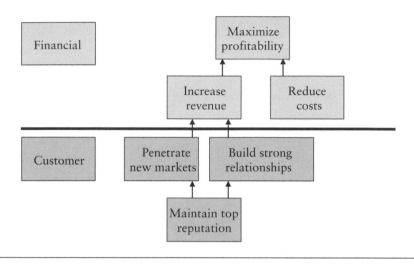

customer objectives and the cost objective. For example, a common principle is that it is less expensive to keep an existing customer versus finding a new one. So if there is an objective of *Build Strong Customer Relationships*, the tendency is to draw the line both into the revenue side and the cost side of the financial equation. While there is nothing technically *wrong* with this practice, it is generally encouraged to only draw an arrow if you believe that accomplishing the lower objective will specifically result in the achievement of the higher objective. In other words, don't get arrow-happy! If the objectives are studied and connections debated long enough, it will certainly be possible to twist logic to the point that every objective could be connected to every other objective. On the other hand, if the process is continued until all objectives are connected and there *still* isn't anything feeding *Reduce Costs*, then it would definitely be a cause for concern. But not having arrows drawn from customer objectives into cost reduction should not be an immediate cause for alarm.

The next step is simply to repeat the process for all remaining perspectives. The given process objectives are *Accelerate Time to Market,*

Optimize Supply Chain, and *Increase On-Time Delivery Percentage.* This is a perfect illustration of why it is necessary to write implications of the facts on the S.W.O.T.s and keep the sticky notes available during map development. For instance, any number of issues could be behind *Optimize Supply Chain* that would affect the group's decision on where the arrows should be drawn. The main theme could be that certain suppliers are unreliable with their delivery times, limiting the organization's ability to *Increase On-Time Delivery Percentage.* Another possibility is that the organization is not taking advantage of volume purchasing due to decentralized ordering, which could result in the failure to *Reduce Costs.* Still another possibility is that there is a link between procuring parts from suppliers in a timely fashion and new product introduction, which would *Accelerate Time to Market.* Several other potential connections could also be made, reinforcing the need to review the sticky notes to determine the original intent.

The other objective might be a bit more straightforward. It seems logical that *Increasing On-Time Delivery Percentage* would be vital to *Building Strong Customer Relationships* and probably *Maintaining a Top Reputation* as well. And *Accelerate Time-to-Market* would logically drive the ability to *Penetrate New Markets* as well as *Building Strong Customer Relationships.* So layering in the Process section could result in the map in Exhibit 4.14.

Note that there are two ways in which the arrows from *Increase On-Time Delivery Percentage* reach *Build Strong Customer Relationships.* One is a direct arrow connecting the two, and the other is an indirect arrow that goes through the intermediate objective of *Maintaining Top Reputation.* This happens fairly often and is not necessarily a logical contradiction. The reasoning in this example is that *Increasing On-Time Delivery Percentage* might well help reputation building, and reputation could certainly in turn help build relationships. But the direct arrow further indicates that there are aspects of building relationships that on-time delivery would solidify that separate from reputation issues.

The positioning of the objectives on the map should be done with an eye toward avoiding the crossing of arrows whenever possible. Sometimes

EXHIBIT 4.14   *Demo Strategy Map: Process Perspective*

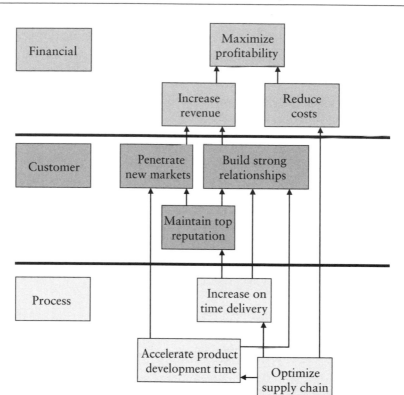

it is unavoidable, but in general the line crosses make the map much harder to read, which limits its effectiveness as a communication tool.

Completing the map involves layering in the Learning and Growth perspective. The objectives presented were *Develop High-Quality Staff*, *Upgrade Systems*, and *Improve Internal Communication*. Learning and Growth objectives also have the characteristic that it will probably be possible to connect them to anything else on the map. There are a few useful techniques available to help minimize confusion, emphasize the most important links, and avoid cluttering the strategy map with dozens of arrows. One is to see if there is a natural hierarchy within the perspective. For example, *Upgrading Systems* could definitely help *Improve*

Internal Communication. In some cases, this connection would be direct and significant enough to simply draw an arrow into the communication objective and let that one feed the objectives in the other perspectives. This would eliminate the need to have multiple connections drawn from every Learning and Growth objective. In this case it would be important to review the sticky notes in the *Upgrade Systems* category to determine how many were communication related. It is likely that there will be too many other issues impacted by technology to simply draw the arrow into communication and be done with it. A more likely result is that *Upgrading Technology* would drive multiple objectives; at Wal-Mart, the electronic distribution process discussed in prior chapters helps *Optimize the Supply Chain.* E-commerce capabilities could also help the organization *Penetrate New Markets.* This list of potential cause-and-effect relationships is long.

The same holds true for *Developing a High-Quality Staff.* It would be a challenge to find an objective on the map that a high-quality staff is *un*related to. The useful technique in this case is to ask the group "If we could only pick one or two objectives to connect *Developing a High-Quality Staff* to, which would they be?" This should give an indication of what the team thinks the training and development priorities should be. The group should also not forget to review the sticky note issues in the staff category, as these could provide insight into which connections would be most valuable. A completed strategy map is illustrated in Exhibit 4.15.

While this map is for demonstration purposes only, there are several interesting observations to be made with regard to the map telling the story of the organization. A company with this map is saying that focusing on systems is of paramount importance. This is evident for two reasons: (1) the verb chosen for the objective is *upgrade*, which clearly implies there's work to be done, and (2) the host of objectives that system upgrades are expected to drive are diverse, significant, and cover all three of the perspectives directly. A question that should immediately be asked upon viewing this map is, "What technology initiatives and budget are being built into the plan?" If there are no activities or budget dollars allocated to technology improvements, this strategy is probably doomed to failure from the start.

EXHIBIT 4.15   *Demo Strategy Map: Learning and Growth Perspective*

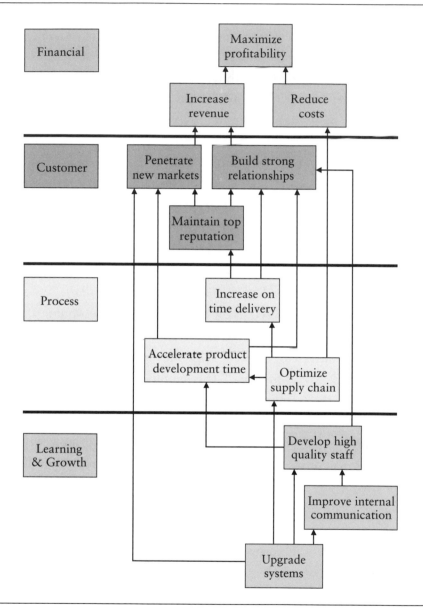

This strategy map also implies that new product development is a significant priority, and it is expected to drive both customer retention and new customer acquisition. Once again, this should prompt an immediate question about what the product development process looks like. The activities needed for execution of this objective could vary widely from company to company. In many organizations a formal research and development department specializes in new products. If this is the case, initiatives to aid in *Accelerating Product Development Time* would most likely involve existing process documentation, analysis, and modification. In short, it might be a standard process improvement team. Other organizations go about product development haphazardly. The process for developing products either doesn't exist or is very informal. These organizations will have to decide whether a more formal approach is needed to develop sufficient products to meet the needs of their strategy.

Another process-related observation is that *Optimize Supply Chain* is the only objective that feeds *Reduce Costs*. This implies one of three possible interpretations:

1. The internal company processes are operating at peak efficiency.
2. The company does not feel that internal process inefficiencies are significant enough to merit mention as part of the strategy.
3. An arrow has been forgotten OR a problem has been discovered; there is an objective of *Increasing On-Time Delivery Percentage*, which would seem to imply process streamlining, but the only arrow coming out of this objective goes into *Build Long Term Relationships*, which is certainly a plausible outcome of increasing delivery reliability. But without the arrow into cost reduction, it leaves open the possibility that expensive means of expediting processes will be employed to get customer orders out faster. If this is the intention of the company, then so be it, but it is an item that should be discussed and agreed to as a management team.

Interpretation discussions such as this are what make a strategy mapping session very valuable for a management team. When properly facilitated, the map really makes the team think about the implications of their actions and do so on a cross-functional basis.

Another key interpretation point can be found in the Customer section. While it is too simplistic to rank the importance of objectives by merely counting the arrows going into and out of them, it is healthy to see a roughly even balance between *Penetrate New Markets* and *Build Strong Long-Term Relationships*. Many companies get so excited about the prospects for growth and new business that they neglect existing customers. The fact that *Develop High-Quality Staff* feeds strong relationships implies that existing customer interface will be an area of focus.

STRATEGY MAP UTILIZATION

A strategy map should not be developed and then locked in a desk drawer or put in a trophy case. Some of the uses for the map (e.g., communication, illustration of cross-functional relationships) have been previously discussed, but additional ongoing uses abound. The next steps in the strategic process post-strategy map are the identification of measures (Balanced Scorecard) and strategic initiatives. These will be covered in detail in subsequent chapters, but suffice it to say that each of the objectives on a strategy map will have measures associated with it. This is mentioned here because *target setting* is an important use for the strategy map.

Where do targets typically come from? Some say past history, statistical projections, and so forth. While this is sometimes true, targets often happen because people pull a number out of thin air and say, "This is what it is going to be." If this is the method for target setting, the strategy map can at least provide a vehicle for helping the organization think about objectives logically. For example, consider the map developed in this section. Target setting should always begin at the top. The number-one objective on the map is to *Maximize Profitability*. Pulling a number out of the air, assume the company has decided that a 10% increase in profitability over the current year is necessary to deem the strategy a success.

The next step is to look at the map to see which objectives feed *Maximize Profitability*. In this case they are *Reduce Costs* and *Increase Revenue*. The management team should question how much of the 10% needed is going to come through revenue generation and how much is going to come through cost reduction. This is a very significant point.

The company might decide that its 50/50—half through more revenue, half through less cost. The company could just as likely decide that revenue should go up 20% and that cost will only go up 10%. (If the latter is the case, the title of the objective should logically be changed from *reduce* to *manage*.) The point is that different initiatives will be necessary in the first case versus the second. If the company determines that a 7% increase in revenue is needed, then the next step is to drop down to the next level and decide how much will come from *Penetrating New Markets* and how much will come from *Building Long-Term Relationships*. And the company must also question if a 3% reduction in cost is possible by *Optimizing the Supply Chain*.

This process continues throughout the diagram. The map gives the leadership team the opportunity to discuss how much impact they think each of the lower-level objectives will have on the objectives they are supposed to support. This can be another very valuable discussion

A further use for the strategy map is at strategic evaluation time. If the company has a Balanced Scorecard that is issued periodically, a meeting should always follow to review the results. If targets are missed, discussing the connections on the strategy map can provide potentially useful cause-and-effect information as to the reason why.

SUMMARY

The strategy map has steadily grown in profile and acceptance since its inception in the early 1990s. This step was skipped by many organizations interested in implementing the Balanced Scorecard. Because the term *scorecard* implied measures, many companies rushed to the measurement part of the process and slapped numbers on things. But the strategy map is a critical precursor to the scorecard because it ensures that the right themes have been identified, that they fit together cohesively, and that all stakeholders understand the direction of the organization.

CHAPTER 5

BALANCED SCORECARD AND STRATEGIC INITIATIVES

The Balanced Scorecard (BSC), like the strategy map, is a tool popularized by Robert Kaplan and David Norton in their series of *Harvard Business Review* articles and books beginning in the early 1990s. The scorecard has gained in popularity over the years and is still seen as a value-added concept almost 15 years after its inception. This certifies that using the Balanced Scorecard has moved beyond fad status and become a popular and accepted business practice. In this chapter the scorecard definition will be presented, followed by examples and an explanation of scorecard development and use. Because strategic initiatives should be identified in parallel with measurement identification, a section on initiative development will follow the discussion of scorecard creation.

DEFINITION

A *Balanced Scorecard* is a management tool that provides senior executives with a comprehensive set of measures to assess how the organization is progressing toward meeting its strategic goals.

There are several important aspects of the definition. The first is that the scorecard is a *management tool*. There are typically two levels of use of a BSC within an organization. Level one is when the scorecard is new and the management team is still trying to figure out how to integrate it into their decision-making system. At this level the scorecard is used by the management team in basically the same way a student views his or her report card in school. The BSC comes out at the end of the grading period, management reviews it and notes that the organization has made twelve targets and missed eight, and so they praise the twelve, chastise the eight, and move on.

At level one the scorecard is usually just one agenda item out of many on the management team meeting agenda, and the person who usually reviews scorecard performance in the management team meeting is the BSC coordinator, not the CEO or president. So the way it usually works is for the big boss to chair the first few agenda items and then say, "Well, Susan, how does the scorecard look this month?" And then Susan says, "Great, Jane. We've made these twelve targets and missed these eight. Back to you." Upon which Jane continues through the remainder of the agenda topics. This is clearly the phase when the management team doesn't really know how to use the scorecard properly as of yet. Every organization goes through level one, but the range of time spent on it can vary widely. Some organizations are through it after one or two scorecard editions, while some never really get through it at all.

Those that are successful break through into level two, where the BSC is truly being used as a *management tool*. There are several significant differences from level one. The first is that the scorecard will not be one agenda item out of many on the management team meeting agenda. Instead, it will drive the agenda. Think about it: If the purpose of the management meeting is to discuss strategy and the future, shouldn't the objectives, measures, and initiatives that the organization deemed vital to strategic success be the drivers of the session? A second difference between levels one and two is the perception of who owns the scorecard during the meeting. In level two, the big boss reviews scorecard performance instead of the coordinator. This raises the perception of importance of the tool in the eyes of everyone at the meeting.

But perhaps the main difference between the levels happens during the discussion of scorecard performance. In level two it is not enough to know that an organization has missed targets, and missing one does not equate to immediate chastising. In level two the focus is on *why* targets were missed. There are a host of reasons that a target might be missed, and each should prompt a different response from the organization. For example, a target might be missed simply because the company is measuring something it has never measured before, so lack of experience with the subject resulted in setting the target unrealistically high. The proper action in this case is simply changing the target to a more realistic level. Another possibility is that the initiatives identified to drive the number in the proper direction are behind schedule, which should prompt rigorous questioning of the team owner(s) by the rest of the management team. Or the initiatives could be on schedule but ineffective for whatever reason. This would represent a learning opportunity for the management team and potentially a change of direction. Still another possibility is that something external has happened to change the business situation. It is possible that a new competitor has entered the market, customers have found new product alternatives, and so forth. The scorecard provides up-to-date information regarding these trends and puts management in the position to determine how to effectively combat them.

Another important aspect of the definition is that the customer of the scorecard is the *executive team*. The definition of the executive team is the group of people ultimately responsible for the business unit for which the scorecard is being created. If the scorecard is of the organization-wide variety, the executive team would be the CEO or President and his or her direct reports; if the scorecard is for the Midwest region of the organization, the executive team would be the head of the Midwest region and his or her direct reports; and if the scorecard is for the IT department, it would be for the head of IT and his or her direct reports. It is important to make this distinction because the primary purpose of the scorecard is to help make sound management decisions, and these are the people that should be making them. The scorecard can certainly be used for communication to the workforce and to illustrate the most important measures, but the main reason the BSC is implemented is to make better management decisions.

The final note on the definition refers to the notion that the scorecard is created to help organizations measure progress toward meeting their *strategic* goals. Often an organization hears "scorecard" and simply starts calling its existing measurement system a Balanced Scorecard. This was common practice for years and still occurs on occasion. The strategy map has helped on this front, since the technique for establishing measures is to use the strategy map objectives as a starting point. The point is that the purpose of the scorecard is to measure progress toward achieving strategy—that is why your organization should do one.

This topic provides an opportunity to clear up some misnomers about the Balanced Scorecard:

- *The BSC doesn't replace all other measurement systems:* The balanced scorecard was not designed as the be-all and end-all of measurement in your organization. Just because you have a BSC does not mean the leadership team cannot look at other data. The BSC is intended to focus on the strategic aspects of the business. There may be a whole host of operational measures the leaders need to manage to as well.

- *Measuring something on a BSC doesn't mean it can't be measured in other places:* A common misconception is that the scorecard must be a unique set of measures. In other words, it should consist of items that are measured *only* on the scorecard. This isn't true. A measure might be valuable from a strategic perspective and useful on the BSC, and also interesting when seen in context with other operational measures. A great example is the Treasury, which keeps track of incoming tax dollars. To claim a BSC measures progress toward achieving a strategy and aids the Treasury in decision making without including tax revenue would be ludicrous, and this number is also vital to making operational decisions regarding today's cash flow.

- *It is not a good thing or a bad thing to be on the BSC . . . it is just a thing:* Sometimes people or departments get upset when they aren't represented on the BSC. They seem to feel that not being on the scorecard makes their department appear less important. A military organization once produced a scorecard that contained around 20 measures, which certainly was a reasonable number. Unfortunately, it turned out that each individual measure was really an index of 10 to 15 other measures, making the scorecard practically impossible to interpret. This happened because each department wanted to make sure they were represented in some fashion on the BSC—and resulted in a product of limited value. Not being on the scorecard doesn't mean you aren't important. It could easily mean that a given department's processes are humming along so efficiently that there's no need for the executive team to spend time talking about them periodically.

  Conversely, some people or departments feel that it is a negative to be represented on the BSC. The implication is that fingers are being pointed at them or that they are being put in the spotlight unfairly. This is certainly not the case either. A given process, for example, might be the key to driving an entirely new revenue stream for the organization. The leadership team might want to discuss the performance of this particular process periodically to ensure they are getting the most out of it. This would definitely not be a negative thing.

  The moral of the story is that the measures that go on the scorecard should be the things that the leadership team needs to discuss on an ongoing basis to determine how they are progressing toward achieving their strategy. This may or may not include Department A, and Department A should not have an automatically positive or adverse reaction in either case.

- *Scorecard measures are not set in stone:* The measurement identification process is inexact. Business conditions change. People get smarter as they learn more about the scorecard and want to see different things. Measures outlive their usefulness. All of these are reasons why an organization shouldn't feel like it is locked in to the exact group of measures that is suggested initially. It is common to have a few measures rotate on or off the scorecard over the course of time. Remember that the objective is to provide management with the information needed for good decision making. If measures need to be added or modified to achieve this objective, then so be it.

- *Each perspective does not need to have the same number of measures:* While it is true that a scorecard wildly out of balance would be a cause for concern, too many organizations waste time trying to have exactly the same number of measures for each perspective. A scorecard with 24 measures does not have to be divided 6-6-6-6. The key is executive interest. If the executives are only interested in four learning and growth measures, for example, it isn't necessary to fill in two more spots with worthless numbers just to balance the number of measures. (This happens more than you might imagine.)

The scorecard has been a valuable tool because it filled a void in the execution of the strategic process. In the pre-BSC world, many organizations would dutifully create a strategic plan every year, present it to their employees, then go back to their real jobs and forget about strategy until the following year—when they would do it again. The scorecard provides a method for keeping the strategy in front of the leadership team over the course of the year. This forces them to make a conscious decision to neglect strategy, as opposed to neglecting it simply because they got too busy with day-to-day issues.

The increase in the speed of business was discussed in Chapter 1. In the good old days, it might have been feasible to create a strategy, let it run for a year, and then revisit it. This practice (in most industries, anyway) will not suffice in today's world; conditions are simply changing too fast. The scorecard provides the vehicle to make the midterm course corrections that are necessary for continued success.

Scorecards can assume many different shapes and sizes. Consider the Treasury example provided in Exhibit 5.1.

EXHIBIT 5.1 *Treasury Balanced Scorecard*

Perspective	Strategic Objective	Lag Measures/ Lead Measures	Target	Actual	Comments
Customer	Increase stakeholder satisfaction	Ind/business taxpayer Student/family	80/80 80/80	73/69 85/85	74 / 67 prior year 76 / 74 prior year
	Promote positive image	Public outreach events	39	27	Special cause low
	Enhance customer communication	Speed of answering phone % call mtg quality stds Written correspondence response time % self-service contacts	5:00m 70% 30 days 90%	6:10m 66% 75 days 87%	CC time Special cause low; new hires Histogram on aging Common cause; 92% avg
Financial	Maintain financial integrity	Credit rating Material audit findings	AAA 0	AAA 3	AAA S&P / AaaMoody / AA+ Fitch Zero repeats
	Generate revenue	GF-GP revenue SAF revenue Enforcement revenue	-6%FY 1.4%FY N/A	-15.1% -1.9% $112.2M	FYTD -9.3% FYTD .5% FYTD $295.4M
	Manage budget	Balanced Budget	<=95%	93%*	*FYTD figure
	Manage investments	Return on investment	8.0%	-7.8%	*Rolling 12 month figure
Process	Streamline key processes	Standardized test TAT Test registration accuracy	10 wks 90%	20 wks 55%	Spring cycle; down from 28

Perspective	Objective	Measure	Target	Actual	Comments
Process (continued)	Minimize early out impact	Sales tax delinquency canc	N/A	27,733	40,253 new issued
		Distressed local gov'ts	N/A	20	3 new, 5 removed (Dec. 02)
		Authority trans prog	4/8	4/8	
		Early out mgmt prog	2/10	2/10	
	Optimize contract management	Contract compliance	100%	92%	
	Increase electronic capabilities	% returns filed by alt means	80%	39%	CYTD 41%
		% electronic disbursements	33%	28%	$5.6B paid; 54% of $ disb
		% electronic state receipts	20%	18%	$5.3B rcvd; 35% of $ rcvd
Learning & Growth	Manage tech resources	% key IT projects on time/ in budget	3.3	2/3	
	Develop positive culture	Employee satisfaction	7.0	4.3	70 employees surveyed
	Improve internal communication	Internal comm events	24	36	
	Provide customer-friendly HR services	Training quality	9.0	9.5	98 attendees, 42 responses
		Hiring cycle time	45 days	52 days	
Security	Improve security	Security breeches	0	0	Software arriving in Jan
		% DR plans tested/app	10/10	0	
		% BC plans tested/app	10/10	0	

There are several important points to be made regarding this example. The first thing to note is the format. Starting on the left-hand side, note that the perspectives follow the same flow and hierarchy that was presented on the Treasury strategy map. Column two contains the objectives, taken directly from the strategy map. This gives the highest probability that scorecard measures will reflect success in achieving the strategy map objectives. Note the positioning of the security objective, placed in the bottom level of the scorecard.

The third column requires a bit of explanation. The topic is measures, and it is segmented into *lag* and *lead* categories. The definition of a *lag* measure is one that reflects an outcome, or result; lags tell you how well you have accomplished something—a reflection of bottom-line results today. A *lead* measure, on the other hand, is one that you would keep track of because you think it will drive positive bottom-line results in the future. A lead might reinforce a certain behavior the organization feels is necessary to achieve the corresponding lag results. For example, a for-profit organization might feel that participation in trade shows is a powerful attractor of new business. Tracking the number of trade shows attended would be considered a *lead* measure. Why? Because the measure is not an end in itself; an organization wouldn't be tracking it to see how many trade shows it could attend. Instead, the attendance would drive a certain outcome, probably something like number of new customers or new customer revenue. These could serve as the corresponding lag measures. Note that in the Treasury example, there are several of each type.

Columns four and five are where the numbers appear. Column four shows the targets for each measure, while column five shows the actual results for the most recent time frame. It is recommended that actual figures be colored according to whether the target has been made or not. Red would indicate a missed target and green would indicate a made one. Some of the numbers may be black, reflecting that a target hasn't been set for that particular category as of yet. Traditional format consists of using the colors of a stoplight to reflect progress (with yellow meaning caution—in danger of missing the target), but this is by no means the only way to do it.

The Treasury example makes the data display as simple as possible: one column for targets, one column for actual numbers. There are a number of variations on this theme. Multiple target columns can be added to reflect year-to-date progress, one-year, two-year, and three-year goals, and so on. The actual column reflects the most recent time frame, but the scorecard can include columns for year-to-date, last month or quarter, same month or quarter last year, rolling 12 months, and so on. Again, there is no perfect format. The best one is the one that helps tell the story of the organization properly so leaders can make effective decisions. The biggest constraint is the space available to tell the story. It is important from a perception perspective to keep the scorecard on one page, so adding too many columns can result in having to use a very small print size!

The right-hand column of the scorecard is reserved for comments. Comments are extremely important in assisting the interpretation of the document. The scorecard should be viewed like the front page of a newspaper. Headlines dominate the front page. If there is an article on the front page, typically only the first few paragraphs are printed before the "See page A17" reference appears at the bottom, directing the reader to jump to another page for the rest of the story. Comments on the scorecard operate exactly the same way. The comments might provide a bit of insight into the headlines (i.e., measures), and they might refer the reader to where further and more detailed information would be available.

There are several instructive points to be made on the content of the Treasury scorecard as well. It was stated previously that the organization has several stakeholder groups. Some of these are spelled out specifically in the measures for the top objective of *Increase Stakeholder Satisfaction*. The first measure is for their most traditional and long-standing customers: the taxpayers. The measure is divided into individual and business to account for the very diverse needs of the two groups.

The second measure is less traditional. The Treasury has a large education component. It oversees the administration of various types of educational grants and funding. So the customers of the education component of the organization have been included, segmented into the students applying for the money and the families of the students applying for the money. Does this mean that other stakeholders aren't important? Of course not, but there are several reasons why these two have been selected for scorecard display. For example, the governor is a key stakeholder in the organization. He was the person the Treasurer reported to, but the Treasurer didn't feel the need to include governor satisfaction as a scorecard measure, stating that "if the governor is unhappy, I'll know it without having to look at a survey!" Other stakeholder groups might be so dynamic and hard to measure that it would be difficult to get meaningful, usable data for them on an ongoing basis. So Treasury settled on the taxpayers and education funding recipients as the BSC-worthy segments.

It should be noted that the satisfaction surveys were conducted annually, while most of the rest of the Treasury numbers are collected quarterly. This should be avoided if at all possible; the time frames for the BSC should be as consistent as you can make them. It makes it much more difficult to interpret results if some numbers are monthly, some are quarterly, annual, and so forth. But in the case of the surveys, it was very time consuming and expensive to get the necessary data. This precluded the possibility of getting quarterly numbers. The numbers were considered to be so important that the leadership team felt it worthwhile to keep them on the scorecard for four successive quarters, regardless of the fact that they weren't changing. Remembering what the satisfaction numbers were and what they wanted them to be was critical in driving decision making.

The following measure is the first lead, entitled *public outreach events*. This is an excellent example of a measure that would be intended to drive a specific result. A public outreach event was an event in which someone from Treasury would go to a local community to inform and educate the taxpayers on the benefits of paying their taxes electronically. Electronic payment definitely could help taxpayers, as electronic refunds would be processed more quickly and the recipients would get their money faster. So this would be a lead measure that could drive individual customer satisfaction. As an added bonus, if a large percentage of taxpayers file electronically, it eases the resource burden on the Treasury staff. Note that in the Process section there is a measure entitled *percentage of returns filed electronically.* The public outreach events, if successful, would drive this percentage higher as well. This would ease the strain on a staff overloaded by two early retirement programs, which was definitely an organizational priority.

The public outreach events measure is therefore not only an example of how lead-lag works, but also an illustration of how lead measures for a given objective may drive measures for other objectives from around the scorecard. A frequently asked question is, "Does each objective have to have a lead and a lag measure associated with it?" What has just been illustrated is that driving relationships may come from other areas, so the answer is no.

Dropping down into the Financial category, the *Generate Revenue* objective also provides the opportunity for analysis. Two of these measures, *GF-GP Revenue* and *SAF Revenue*, were long-standing measures within the organization. They dealt with the funds coming in from the general fund and the school fund. While Treasury was responsible for *managing* to these numbers, they did not *control* these numbers. In other words, it wasn't up to the Treasury to increase taxes, but it collected the additional taxes after they were raised. The important point here is that an *organization does not have to be able to control every measure on its scorecard.* Executive teams are sometimes reluctant to include measures on their scorecard that they cannot control, particularly if their compensation is involved. But the objective of the scorecard is to make good management decisions, and if a measure as important as *GF-GP Revenue* measure was not a part of the Treasury scorecard, then nobody would take it seriously as a management tool.

The *enforcement revenue* measure completes the *Generate Revenue* objective and is a good complement to the other two. This measure consisted of the sum total collected through discovery, audit, and collections—three things that *were* within the Treasury's control. Looking at these three measures together gave the management team a good understanding of the revenue picture.

Another reason *enforcement revenue* is instructive is due to the lack of a target. There are many reasons why a target might not be added to a scorecard. One is simply that the category is so new that it is difficult to hazard a guess as to what a reasonable target might be, so the company prefers to wait until getting data to set one. But that wasn't the issue in this case. Another possibility is that the topic is beyond the control of the organization, so setting a target would be pointless. (*Note:* The GF-GP Revenue and SAF Revenue have targets even though they are out of Treasury's control, but these were set externally and included so Treasury could see how the measures shaped up.) But that wasn't the issue in this case either. The issue here was public perception. It would send a wrong message to the public for their Treasury to have a target for audit, for example. This would imply that they would keep looking until they find something, and then they would stop.

Note the *Streamline Key Processes* objective in the Process section. The procedure Treasury decided to follow was to select a key process from each area that had strategic significance and put measures on the BSC. The first two processes measured came from the Education department and focused on the handling of the state standardized test scores. This came as no surprise to anyone, because this process was constantly in the public eye and scrutinized by the media. The surprise came from the tax division. The process selected was relatively obscure, but had far-reaching resource implications. The measure selected was *sales tax delinquency cancellations*. Basically all it meant was that if a business didn't pay its taxes, Treasury was responsible for going out and getting them. This was called a sales tax delinquency assessment. But there are several reasons why the assessment may be issued incorrectly as the result of an internal process issue. For example, the business could have changed its name and paid under the new name, but the collections department wasn't informed in time. Or the business could have moved and paid from the new address, and the collections department wasn't informed in time. Or the business could have been acquired and paid under the acquiring company's name, and the collections department wasn't informed in time. If the collection agent found any of these to be true and that the business was paid up to date, then the assessment would be cancelled. The volume of these (over 27,000) that occurred in the prior quarter convinced management that a significant portion of resources were being consumed that could perhaps be better used preventing incorrect assessments from being issued in the first place. This is an excellent example of how the BSC process can bring issues to light that otherwise may go unnoticed and cause problems for the organization.

Note that the remainder of the objectives and measures in the Process category are aimed at the same process efficiency targets in the *Streamline Key Processes* objective. *Early Out* was the name of the early retirement program that was eliminating a healthy percentage of the workforce. The measure for minimizing the impact of early out was simply *Early Out Management (progress versus plan)*. The Treasury had a management committee that met regularly that was in charge of properly managing the Early Out program. This committee had developed a timeline with tight milestones, designed to minimize disruption of service as much as possible during the transition. A target of 4/8 in this case represents that, according to the timeline, four out of the eight milestones were to have been achieved by the current issue of the scorecard. Since 4/8 appears in the actual column as well, the initiative is on target.

This isn't the most revealing of measures. The fact that the initiative is on target does not indicate whether it will be ultimately successful, so there may be limited value in an activity check measure such as this. But if the objective is to give the leadership team the information they need to make good decisions, and the progress of this committee is an issue that needs frequent discussion, having it on the front page won't do any damage. It is important to note, however, that progress of *all* initiatives cannot be documented on the front page of the BSC. If they were, the scorecard would be nothing but a list of activities, and meaningful interpretation would be next to impossible.

The Learning and Growth objective also contains interesting information. One of the measures is *internal communication events*. The purpose of this measure was to reinforce certain management behaviors. Many organizations have trouble with programs that start off riding a wave of interest, then fizzle out once the initial excitement wears off. Treasury did not want that to happen with its Balanced Scorecard efforts. It defined an internal communication event as a communication session between a member of the executive team together with employees from multiple areas, conducted specifically to discuss balanced scorecard, strategic plan, or budget. In this way they constantly reinforced their commitment to these topics and got a chance to hear what the workforce had to say as well.

A cynic might doubt the usefulness of the communication events measure. The manager in question might not be taking it seriously, might do a horrible job presenting the strategic perspective due to lack of preparation, might refer to a regular meeting as a communication event just to meet the required number, and so forth. In short, there are a lot of ways to monkey around with the number. But something important to remember is that *any* measure can be tinkered with, if that is the intent of the leadership team. If the objective is to get out and discuss strategy with the workforce and then carry the insights gained back to the leadership team, then this measure would be successful.

This scorecard was merely a first-edition demo that was presented to the Treasury executives. Generally speaking, the executive team is responsible for the objectives column of the scorecard. Then the executives hand off development responsibilities to what is known as the *implementation team*. This team includes employees from around the organization who have a collective understanding of the BSC perspectives as they apply to the company. This group also needs to be able to figure out what to measure and where to go to get the data to measure it. The Treasury scorecard development was ultimately successful because their implementation team was large, talented, dedicated, and diverse.

Having said this, the first draft still has some areas for improvement. For example, the best measure the team came up with for *Provide Customer-Friendly HR Services* was *training quality*, measured by average evaluation score on post-class training. This type of measure is notoriously unreliable and probably destined to be replaced. *Employee satisfaction* was measured through internal focus groups versus formal survey, so the accuracy of this measure should be called into question as well. It is not unusual for a team to struggle at first when trying to identify good learning and growth measures. This area typically has been measured the least, especially from an executive level. Trial and error is to be expected.

A for-profit BSC example comes from Orion Development Group and is illustrated in Exhibit 5.2, with numbers changed to protect the organization's privacy.

Format differences abound between this example and the Treasury example. Starting on the left, note that there is no separate column for perspectives; they are listed inside the objectives column. Also note that instead of having a measures column that offsets lag and lead, this version has a separate column that labels each measure as one or the other. There are data columns for actual and target just like in the Treasury example, but this scorecard also includes columns for year-to-date actuals and targets. The final difference is the column on the far right, designating an owner for each measure. The purpose of the owner is to make sure that data for the measure finds it way onto the BSC. This does *not* mean that the owner is responsible for collecting it; the responsibility is simply to make sure it *gets* collected. The reason such emphasis is being placed on this point is that the owner of each measure should be a member of the executive team, so the senior executive doesn't have far to look to find the accountable person if a measure isn't properly prepared for the BSC. (*Note:* The comments column of the scorecard was not presented due to space restrictions.)

In terms of content, several measures provide interesting learning points. A good example of the lag-lead balance can be found in the Customer perspective in the *Strengthen Existing Customer Relationships* objective. The lead measure of *cross-sell customer visits* was defined as the number of times a person or team from the organization called on an existing customer to discuss what other Orion services might be useful to them. Before this measure could be implemented, it would be necessary to perform an analysis of existing customers, the services they buy, and the potential services they would benefit from. Once the potential needs were established, the proper expertise would be assembled to

EXHIBIT 5.2 *ODG Balanced Scorecard*

Strategic Objective	Measures	Type	Qtr Target	Qtr Actual	YTD Target	YTD Actual	Owner
Financial							
Maintain strong $ position	Net profit	Lag	$100K	$53K	$300K	$319	PK
Increase revenue	Service line revenue	Lag	$200K	$157k	$600K	$657	PK
	Public seminar revenue	Lag	$300K	$308k	$900K	$980K	PK
	In-house revenue	Lag	$200K	$198k	$600K	$500k	PK
Customer							
Strengthen existing customer relationships	Repeat business revenue	Lag	$500K	$479K	$1.5M	$1.6M	BB
	% multi-product customers	Lag	40%	37%	-40%	37%	BB
	Cross-sell customer visits	Lead	6	2	18	7	MD
Attract new clients	New client revenue	Lag	$200k	$184	$600k	$537	PK
	Articles published	Lead	2	-1	6	5	SW
Manage university network	# key markets underserved	Lead	0	3	0	3	PK
	Leads generated via seminar follow up	Lead	8	10	24	22	PK
Establish Orion brand	Post-contract client satisfaction	Lead	95%	99%	95%	99%	MD

Establish Orion brand (continued)	Client-initiated process imps	Lead	3	0	9	1	SW
Process							
Improve sales processes	Executive contacts	Lead	6	8	18	18	MD
	Proposal hit ratio	Lag	60%	50%	60%	30%	MD
Expand product lines	# new products introduced	Lead	3	4	9	6	BB
Develop alternative marketing channels	# public seminars offered	Lead	30	28	90	75	PK
	Public seminars with >18 participants	Lag	25	12	75	61	PK
	Marketing cost as %	Lag	25%	28%	25%	26%	PK
Standardize service delivery	% acceptable audits	Lead	100%	75%	100%	88%	PK
Learning & Growth							
Optimize consulting staff quality	% consultants certified	Lead	100%	100%	100%	100%	MD
	Seminars attended for continuing education	Lead	10	2	30	16	MD
Improve int communication	Database updated and accessible	Lead	yes	yes	N/A	N/A	SW

ensure the company representatives could speak intelligently to the customers about what the new services were and why they needed them. This is why the visit might necessitate a team versus an individual. This activity created a win-win situation even when no new services were purchased because it showed customers that Orion was looking out for their needs (versus the hit-and-run mentality of many of their competitors). When the cross-sell visits were successful in selling more service, the corresponding lag measure of *percentage of multi-product customers* rose.

The measures for *Establish Orion Brand* may seem unconventional for that particular category, but the organization felt that differentiating itself from competitors was a key to success, and tried to determine what would establish Orion as a breed apart. *Post-contract client satisfaction* was a measure created to make sure the company followed up after services were rendered to ensure complete satisfaction and maintenance of the gains made. The thinking was that truly satisfied customers would not only stick with Orion, but also provide invaluable references in the marketplace. And *client-initiated process improvements* was a measure designed to encourage Orion staff to listen to what customers were saying post-engagement and take action to improve the service delivery process to make it more client-focused. Again, it was felt that this would help differentiate the company in the marketplace.

In the Process perspective under *Improve Sales Processes,* there is a lead measure of *executive contacts*. The company has a desire to deal with decision makers in client organizations. They feel it speeds up the process, ensures that deliverables are clear from beginning to end, and increases the probability that necessary resources will be available for the client to implement internal improvements. *Executive contacts* was a count of the new prospect companies in which the sales organization was able to establish the relationship with upper management versus low or nonmanagement as the primary contact point. Several potential initiatives were identified to increase the probability of accessing the organizational leaders.

The Learning and Growth perspective provides a few interesting learning points as well. The *percentage of consultants certified* reflected how well the organization was preparing its new people to deliver the material "the Orion way." Given the aforementioned nature of its business (consultants paid by the day while maintaining separate practices on the side), this was a tremendous challenge—but necessary to achieve upstream objectives. The final measure was an interesting case in that it was purely qualitative. A database was being created that included up-to-date client information, industry experience of the consulting staff, and the like. Everything a traveling service provider with the company needed to know to be successful. The development of this database was a long-term project that the Orion leadership team did not want to let slide. The managing partner was responsible for providing a "yes" or "no" for the scorecard each reporting period, letting the rest of the leadership team know if progress on the database had been satisfactory in the prior reporting period. While this was definitely unscientific, it ensured the leadership team would talk about the issue during scorecard review.

BALANCED SCORECARD: IMPLEMENTATION

Putting together a Balanced Scorecard is much easier once the strategy map has been created. The first few columns of the BSC that deal with perspectives and objectives are already completed on the strategy map and can easily be formatted. Recalling the example from the mock strategy map developed in the previous chapter, the left-hand side of the scorecard appears as shown in Exhibit 5.3.

The next step is to identify and prioritize measures. This is the primary responsibility of the *implementation team*, discussed early in this chapter. The team should follow the process illustrated in Exhibit 5.4 to aid in measurement identification and prioritization.

The first step the team must take sounds very straightforward: select an objective to identify measures for. While seemingly simple, a few basic ground rules should help get the process off to a good start:

- *Pick something simple:* Never start with an objective for which it will be difficult to identify measures. Objectives that are focused on

EXHIBIT 5.3 *Demo Balanced Scorecard: Perspectives and Objectives*

Perspective	Strategic Objective	Lag Measures/ Lead Measures	Target	Actual	Comments
Financial	Maximize profitability				
	Increase revenue				
	Reduce costs				
Customer	Build strong cust relationships				
	Penetrate new markets				
	Maintain top reputation				
Process	Increase on-time delivery %				
	Accelerate product development time				
	Optimize supply chain				
Learning & Growth	Develop high-quality staff				
	Improve internal comm.				
	Upgrade systems				

communication, technology, culture, or any behavioral-sounding issues have been historically difficult to measure. These should be avoided until the team has gained some experience with the process. Starting with objectives like *Penetrate New Markets* or *Increase On-Time Delivery Percentage* will get the meeting off to a good start.

EXHIBIT 5.4   *Measurement Development*

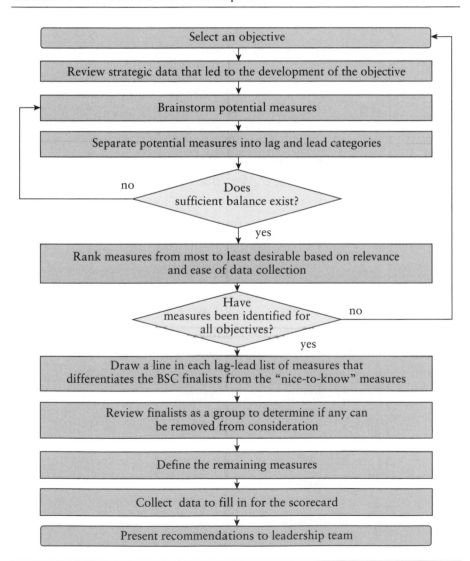

- *Avoid financial objectives:* While there should be a person or two on the implementation team who intimately understands financials, the language of finance is something not every employee understands. Beginning with financial objectives generally results in one or two group members doing all the talking and making all the decisions while everyone else watches and listens. It might even be advisable for the finance experts to identify the top financial measures separately, fit them to the given objectives, and present them to the rest of the team. This greatly expedites the process.

The second step of the process is to review the strategic data that led to the development of the chosen objective. This means that the implementation team must have access to the S.W.O.T. list of issues prepared and sorted by the executive team. This is very important. During the process of naming the objectives, the executives summarized dozens of issues with very short verb-noun titles. The implementation team needs to do an issue review to ensure the key points made by the executives are understood in each category. This could also assist in brainstorming measures. For example, if an opportunity under *Penetrate New Markets* was to market services throughout Canada to attract new customers, then potential BSC measures might be Canadian sales dollars, number of Canadian customers, and so on.

After reviewing the strategic issues under the objective, the next step is to brainstorm potential measures. The most important ground rule is to follow proper brainstorming procedure. In other words, *don't* evaluate each idea as it is mentioned. Some team members have a tendency to start commenting "How would you measure that?" or "That isn't really a measure" and so forth. If this happens, the brainstorming will take an inordinately long time. There is also a risk that team members will feel criticized and they will shut down, causing you to lose the opportunity to find the best combination of measurement possibilities. The facilitator should continue to ask for possibilities and keep the team focused on generation versus evaluation until a good list of possibilities is created. Ideally, each measure will be listed on a sticky note and grouped on a flipchart page. If *Penetrate New Markets* was the selected objective, the resulting list of measures may look like the list in Exhibit 5.5.

Once the possibilities have all been documented, the next step is to separate the measures into the lag and lead categories. Recall that lag measures reflect outcomes, or bottom-line results *today*. Lead measures drive bottom-line results in the future. Ground rules to help with the sorting are as follows:

- *Pick the easy ones first:* Usually, about 60% to 70% of the measures will be easy to categorize. Zero in on a few of those first, and get as many as you can categorized as quickly as possible. It is important to get the categorization rolling and make progress before bogging down into long-winded discussion of one or two measures.

- *Don't obsess over the categorization:* The remainder of the measures will be grey zone issues; they could be lag or lead, depending on the team member's point of view. A very important facilitation tip is to not spend more than a few minutes discussing any one measure. If a decision cannot be reached within a few minutes and the arguments for lag and lead both have merit, write the measure twice and move on.

EXHIBIT 5.5 *Potential Measures for Penetrate New Markets*

Canadian sales dollars	# of new markets entered	Market potential analysis	# of new customers	# Gold markets identified	# of new products

New market sales $	Trade shows attended	Quality prospect visits	New customer satisfaction	Total revenue	New customer hit ratio

- *Recognize when items are actually initiatives:* In the list of potential measures provided, there was an item entitled *market potential analysis.* This could be an example of a one-time initiative versus an ongoing measure. It is common to encounter a few of these during each brainstorming session. These ideas should not be discarded; keep them in a separate column for later discussion. While it is typically the responsibility of the leadership team to identify strategic initiatives, it is fine for the implementation team to recommend the top few initiative opportunities that result from their brainstorming. As an example, the implementation team at the Treasury identified around 100 potential initiatives during their measurement brainstorming. They selected the dozen or so they liked the most and presented these to the leadership team. Roughly half were approved and initiated on the spot.

Following these ground rules could result in a categorization as shown in Exhibit 5.6.

It is instructive to examine the list and discuss the categorization in case the thinking is not obvious. A measure like *new market sales dollars* is obviously a lag. It is the ultimate reflection of how well the organization has penetrated new markets. *Number of new customers* is basically the same measure, but expressed in numbers versus dollars. (*Note:* There will be definitional decisions to be made when clarifying the number of new customers. For example order to truly reflect how well new markets have been penetrated, the company may wish to restrict the count of new customers to those only in previously unserved markets. In other words, new customers in existing markets might not count as part of the measure.)

A measure such as *quality prospect visits* would clearly be a lead. The reason is that this measure is not an outcome in itself, so the company would not measure this with the objective of seeing how many visits they could make. Rather, the objective would be to make the visits to drive an intended result: new customer dollars, number of new customers, and many of the other candidates on the lag list. The same logic

EXHIBIT 5.6   *Sorted Measures for Penetrate New Markets*

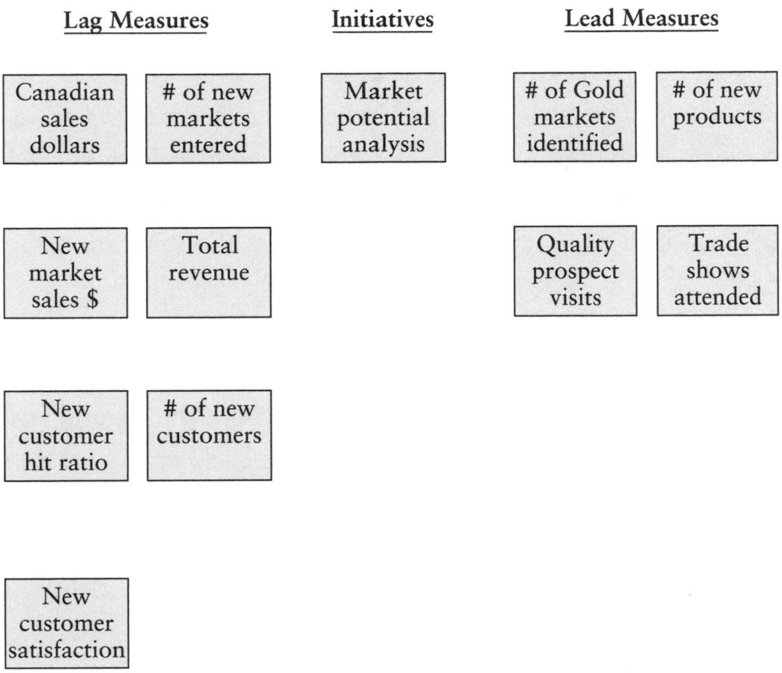

Lag Measures		Initiatives	Lead Measures	
Canadian sales dollars	# of new markets entered	Market potential analysis	# of Gold markets identified	# of new products
New market sales $	Total revenue		Quality prospect visits	Trade shows attended
New customer hit ratio	# of new customers			
New customer satisfaction				

would apply to *trade shows attended*. Note that another one of the lead measures is *number of gold markets identified*. Natural question: What is a gold market? The answer: whatever the company wants it to be. It is possible to define a gold market as one in which a certain sales potential exists, is within a certain geographic region, and so forth. The parameters can be established by the organization. This could be an excellent lead measure for two reasons: It isolates the most potentially profitable market opportunities, and it is memorable. Once the term gold markets is accepted in the organization, the management team will remember to continue trying to find and exploit them because the name keeps the measure top-of-mind.

A few measures on the list are harder to classify. A good example is *new customer satisfaction*. One argument could be to make this a lag measure because satisfaction will not be tracked until someone has already become a customer. Therefore the penetration has already been completed. Another argument could be that *keeping* the customer is the real issue, because penetration doesn't occur if the customer leaves right away. Both of these arguments have merit. The important thing is not to waste an hour discussing and debating to determine which argument is right. Pick one after a few minutes and move on. Note the positioning of *market potential analysis*, classified as an initiative and placed in the separate column in the middle.

At this point, the flowchart asks the question of whether a good balance exists between lag and lead. This is about quality versus quantity. If there are a few good scorecard candidates in both the lag and lead categories, then move on to the next step. If not, cycle back and do more focused brainstorming on the category that needs more possibilities. This will almost always be the lead category, as team members will naturally focus on lag. A useful facilitation question to help identify more lead possibilities would be, "What can we do to help us penetrate new markets?" This might generate additional lead possibilities such as *advertising dollars spent* or *product demos conducted*, which would then be added to the lead list.

The next step is to rank the measures from most to least desirable, based on relevance and ease of data collection. In other words, this is the time to start trying to determine which of the measures is important enough to be on the scorecard. Beginning with the lag list, ask the question, "If there were only one lag measure on the Balanced Scorecard for *Penetrate New Markets*, which one would it be?" This question clearly establishes *relevance* as the primary criteria for prioritization versus *ease of data collection*. This is as it should be. Ease of data collection should be used to break the tie only if two measures are tied on relevance. Once the tie is broken, determine which of the remaining measures would go next, again based on relevance. Continue the process until all measures are ranked. Repeat the process for the lead measures. The result of this activity will look something like the list in Exhibit 5.7.

EXHIBIT **5.7** *Ranked Measures for Penetrate New Markets*

Lag Measures   Lead Measures

| New market sales $ | | Quality prospect visits |

| Number of new customers | | Number of gold markets identified |

| New customer hit ratio | | Trade shows attended |

| Number of new markets entered | | Number of new products |

| New customer satisfaction |

| Total revenue |

| Canadian sales $ |

Ground rules assisting in the ranking are as follows:

- *Look for measures that are really subsets of other measures: Canadian sales dollars* is really just a subset of the *new market dollars* measure. Having both on the scorecard wouldn't be justified unless the Canadian market was deemed so important that it needed to be viewed separately. In this case it was simply moved to the bottom of the list since it would be incorporated into the other measure anyway.

- *Remember other objectives may be more relevant to certain measures: Total revenue* was ranked very low on the lag side. This isn't because it isn't an important measure, and it almost certainly would be one of the finalists for the scorecard. It will probably show up as a high-priority measure under the *Increase Revenue* objective, which seems a more natural fit. If the main ranking criterion is relevance, total revenue will not be a high-ranking issue under *Penetrate New Markets*; new market revenue would be combined with existing market revenue in this measure, and the ability to interpret market penetration would be lost. Likewise, *new customer satisfaction* might be a subset of a *customer satisfaction* measure under the objective *Build Strong Customer Relationships*.

- *Don't spend a lot of time ranking after the first three or four:* The next step after the measures are ranked will be to determine which will be candidates for the final BSC. Because there are only 20 to 25 measures on a standard scorecard, it is highly unlikely that any candidates ranked below the top few for a given objective will make the final BSC. Many teams spend an inordinate amount of time trying to decide which lag measure should go seventh on the list and which should go eighth, but since neither will make the scorecard, this is an irrelevant discussion. Spend time ranking the top four or so, and then do the rest quickly.

The timing of the process to this point will be roughly 30 minutes per objective. This is an average; the financial objectives will be much shorter, and the behavioral, technology, and communication issues will probably take longer. Note that the next step in the process is the question of whether measures have been identified for all objectives. If the answer is no, the team should pick another objective and repeat the process on a new flipchart page until all objectives have a set of ranked measures.

Figuring 30 minutes per objective and a total of around a dozen objectives, the measurement identification process will take roughly a full day. It is strongly recommended that the implementation team get this done in one continuous meeting if possible. If the measurement identification is split up into six or seven one-hour sessions, no momentum is generated and the process takes too long. Plus, the identification process is a great day's work for a team that is just getting started.

After each objective has ranked measures, the next step of the process is to draw a line in each lag-lead list of measures that differentiates the scorecard finalists from the "nice to know" measures. In other words, look at the measures and decide which would be serious candidates for the top 20 to 25 measures for the scorecard. If the team felt that only the top two measures fit this mold, a line would be drawn under the second measure. The same process would be repeated for the lead measures. An example is illustrated for the previously determined *Penetrate New Markets* objective in Exhibit 5.8.

Drawing the lines in the locations shown would indicate that the team felt that a total of five measures from this objective were serious candidates for the Balanced Scorecard. Multiplying that by roughly a dozen objectives would yield about 60 measures making it through this round of prioritization. This is fairly common and should be taken as a sign of progress. The team can typically begin with an infinite number of possibilities and narrow it down to 50 or 60 or so in one day. The next step is a critical one: reviewing the finalists as a group to determine if any can be removed from consideration. At the end of the prior step, all of the above-the-line measures should be grouped together as shown in Exhibit 5.9.

This template contains roughly 65 measures, which is representative of what will come out of the prior step. It is well worth the time to now review the measures to see which do not seem important enough to proceed with. Ground rules for this step are as follows:

- *Look for identical measures in different categories:* Training is a classic example. Often teams will brainstorm lead measures for training in several different categories. In the previous example, training is listed as a potential measure for customer service, on-time delivery performance, new product development, and staff development. The team may wish to identify the one objective

EXHIBIT 5.8   *Determination of BSC Finalists*

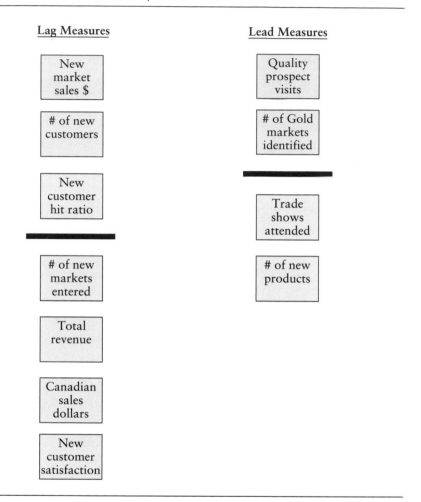

where these possibilities would best fit and group them under one measure in that spot. In this case, *Develop High-Quality Staff* seems like a logical place for all the training measures to be grouped. A top-line measure of *training days* could be supplemented by a definition that only counts training in the aforementioned areas if the team desired.

EXHIBIT 5.9 *"Above-the-Line" Measurement Candidates*

Strategic Objectives	Lag Measures	Lead Measures
Financial		
• Maximize profitability	ROE, ROI, EPS, EVA, net profit, share price	
• Increase revenue	Gross revenue	
• Reduce costs	SG&A, cost per unit, admin expense	
Customer		
• Build strong cust relationships	Share of account, cross sell ratio, customer retention, market share, # lost customers	Value-added services, incentives paid, pref supp, cust service training
• Penetrate new markets	New customer $, new customers, new customer hit ratio	# quality prospect visits, Gold market identified
• Maintain top reputation	New customers, new business $, Positive media mentions	Seminars held, quality contacts, advertising $
Processes		
• Increase on-time delivery %	On-time delivery %, penalties paid, reasons for lateness	Training days
• Accelerate product development time	New product sales, on-target product intros, cycle time, new product profitability	Product development training, R&D budget as % of sales, ideas vetted, ideas approved, products in pipeline
• Optimize supply chain	Stockouts, penalties received, BI's	# preferred suppliers, total # suppliers
Learning and Growth		
• Develop high-quality staff	Profit per ee	ee satisfaction, # training days, open positions, turnover
• Improve internal comm.	Communication Survey results	Communication events, int cust/supp workshops, # of meetings, intranet hits
• Upgrade systems	System downtime	e-orders, tech $ as % of budget, first call resolution, technology training days

- *Look for measures that are restated versions of other measures:* This is often the case. Under the *Build Strong Customer Relationships* objective, there are two lag measures of *customer retention* and *number of lost customers.* One of these can be stated as an inverse of the other, so it is an open question whether both would be needed on the scorecard. This would probably represent another opportunity for consolidation.

- *Beware of measures that sound like they will need to be expanded to show multiple categories:* The objective *Increase On-Time Delivery Percentage* has an associated measure of *reasons for lateness.* It is difficult to envision how this would fit on a scorecard without listing several reasons and how often each occurred. The problem is that one measure could easily expand to several and take up a large portion of the scorecard. With few exceptions, it is practically impossible to show multiple categories of the same measure on the front page of a scorecard.

  However, there is a creative way to get the information on the front page without taking up too much space. For example, assume an organization wanted to keep track of product sales by region. Putting six regions on the scorecard might be impractical. However, if the organization has targets for sales in each region, the measure could be changed to *# of underperforming regions* (or number of RED regions if you would like a more memorable name). That way if the number in the actual column for the month or quarter was a "1," then management would know there was one region not performing as projected. This region could be listed in the comments column so management could ask the appropriate questions.

- *Beware of measures that are clearly annual:* The *Build Strong Customer Relationships* objective has a *market share* measure attached. In some industries this is so difficult to measure that the numbers are only gathered annually. If the measure isn't needed to make crucial decisions or not deemed important enough to keep on a monthly or quarterly scorecard even when it isn't changing (like the taxpayer satisfaction measures on the Treasury scorecard), then removing this one from consideration now could save time later.

- *Question whether the most senior executive needs to know the measure to run the company properly:* A great prioritization technique is to view the customer of the scorecard as one person, not the entire executive team. The ultimate customer is the CEO or President. When deciding whether a measure should remain on the list, determine whether the measure in question is one the CEO needs to know to run the organization properly. If it isn't, then remove it from the list. If the customer is viewed as the entire leadership team, then prioritization will be much more difficult. The team will reason that "the CFO wants to see these 15 measures, and the CIO wants to see these 12, and the COO wants to see these 19," and the result will be that it will be impossible to determine a manageable number of measures.

  In the given example, measures in the Learning and Growth perspective such as *number of meetings held* and *intranet hits* may not really be of interest to a senior executive (at least not of interest relative to all the other possibilities) and could be removed.

The team should spend a good deal of time applying the ground rules and evaluating the measures. The next step in the process is very time consuming, so removing a healthy percentage of the measures at this stage is usually time well spent. The conclusion of the review could yield the table in Exhibit 5.10.

This diagram shows that the total number of measures has been trimmed to under 30. This is probably on the optimistic side. Usually an hour or two of analysis can help narrow the total number of possibilities down from the original 60 or so to around 40 or so, and these are the measurement candidates to be carried on to the measurement definition phase of the process.

EXHIBIT 5.10   *Measurement Candidates after Prioritization*

Strategic Objectives	Lag Measures	Lead Measures
Financial •Maximize profitability •Increase revenue •Reduce costs	ROE, net profit Gross revenue SG&A	
Customer •Build strong cust relationships •Penetrate new markets •Maintain top reputation	Cross sell ratio, customer retention New customers, new cust hit % Positive media mentions	Pref supplier designations, # quality prospect visits, Gold markets identified Seminars held
Processes •Increase on-time delivery % •Accelerate product development time •Optimize supply chain	On-time delivery % Cycle time, new product profitability BI's	R&D budget as % of sales, products in pipeline # preferred suppliers
Learning and Growth •Develop high quality staff •Improve internal comm. •Upgrade systems	Profit per ee	# training days, # open positions, turnover Communication events e-orders, tech $ as % of budget

Measurement definition can be time consuming and frustrating, but it is without question one of the most important parts of scorecard development. This is the step in which the measures must be precisely clarified, to determine what counts as part of the measure and what does not. Normally, during this step it becomes evident that certain measures cannot be quantified or displayed in a meaningful way, leading to them being removed from consideration. Thus, the definition process can serve as another measurement screen. A sample measurement definition from a state Department of Management and Budget is shown in Exhibit 5.11.

There are several components of note in the definition. Any good measurement definition will need to include the following:

- *Context of the measure (which strategic perspective and objective did it come from?):* In the given example, it is explained at the top that this particular measure comes from the process perspective and from an objective entitled *Deliver Quality IT Services.*

EXHIBIT 5.11   *Sample Measurement Definition*

BSC Perspective: Process

BSC Strategic Category: **Deliver Quality IT Services**

Measure: **Percentage of ITSD Support Desk Problems Resolved on the First Contact**

Definition: Of the total number of contacts regarding problems received by the ITSD support desk, the percent resolved on the first contact. A contact is considered resolved if a user problem/question is taken care of or a request that requires action from another unit properly handled/referred (e.g. on a request to order equipment, the help desk would generate the order and consider the contact resolved)

Data: Support desk information collected by ITSD and reported to the BSC coordinator. ITSD prepares monthly reports that represent an average of the individual technician statistics. The monthly reports are averaged to calculate the quarter and year to date percentages. *Relates to SPLAN 5C Deliver Quality IT Services*

Appearing on BSC: Percentage of ITSD support desk problem calls resolved on the first call — Quarter and YTD

Example:

	Quarter	YTD
Total Tickets	500	2410
Tickets Resolved	300	1586
% Resolved 1st Level	60%	65.8%

Resolved on first contact: Quarter 60%   Year to Date 65.8%

Answering problem calls on the first call minimizes customer downtime and frustration, **increasing customer satisfaction** and aids in **maximizing value** to the customer.

- *A paragraph explaining what counts as part of the measure and what does not:* The definition paragraph is an attempt to introduce and clarify key terms and clear up any potential ambiguity. This example explains what a contact is, what resolved means, and so forth.

- *A paragraph explaining how the data will find its way onto the scorecard:* The data paragraph explains who will collect the data, where they will send it, and so forth. In this example, ITSD will collect the data and forward it to the BSC coordinator, who will be responsible for connecting it to strategic plan activity.
- *An explanation (with an example) of how the data will be calculated and displayed on the scorecard:* It is very insightful to try to work through a calculation of the measure being defined, even if the data is fictitious. It forces the group to think through the calculation of the number and whether it will make sense in a scorecard format. Thinking through the numbers often forces modifications to the definition that ultimately improve the scorecard product.
- *An explanation of how the measure winds through the strategy map cause-and-effect arrows to impact the overall number-one objective of the organization:* Questions are inevitable when the implementation team makes recommendations to the executive team. The most common question asked is, "Why are we measuring this?" or "Why should we care about this?" The rectangular box outlined in black at the bottom of the definition helps the implementation team prepare to answer that question. The purpose of the box is to track the measure through its strategy map connections all the way to the top objective on the map. In this example, the help desk measure was under the *Deliver High-Quality IT Services* objective, which was in the Process section. This objective drove an objective in the Customer section entitled *Increase Customer Satisfaction,* which in turn drove the overall number-one objective of *Maximize Value to the Customer.* If it is a chore to clarify the connection of a measure to the overall number-one objective, it may be a sign that the measure isn't really aligned with the strategy and needs to be modified.

Measurement definition is not easy to do. In fact, even skilled practitioners will find that creating a document like the one in Exhibit 5.11 can easily take an hour or more. It is easy to see why coming into the definition phase with 60 measures is not a great situation. This reinforces the need to study the measurement finalists and prune out the ones that you feel are not really serious candidates to make the final scorecard.

The process for measurement definition is illustrated in Exhibit 5.12.

After selecting a measure to define, a good technique is to list all the questions that must be answered or issues that must be resolved to have a measure that is well-defined. For example, one of the measures for the *Penetrate New Markets* objective in the sample is *new customer dollars*. In order to define this measure properly, questions that would have to be answered include the following:

- "What is a *new* customer?"
- "How long will a customer be considered new for scorecard purposes?"
- "Is there a statute of limitations?" (In other words, if a customer bought something many years ago and then stopped, would they be considered new again after a certain amount of time has passed?)
- "Will the dollars be recorded on the BSC in the month the contract is signed or prorated over the life of the contract?"
- "Is there a minimum dollar value to be considered for scorecarding purposes, or does any purchase by a customer count?"

EXHIBIT 5.12   *Measurement Definition Process*

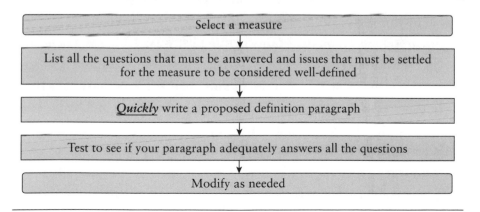

The list of questions might be much longer, but these will do for illustration purposes. The next step is to choose one person in the group to *quickly* write a proposed definition paragraph that addresses the questions posed. Notice that in the flowchart the word *quickly* is underlined, highlighted, and italicized. It is extremely important not to try to write something absolutely perfect the first time. Experience has shown that this will take far longer than the recommended approach. Instead, have someone in the group take his or her best shot at a good definition, quickly writing something like:

> New customer dollars will be counted as those dollars received from any customer that is making their first purchase ever from our organization. The total dollar value of the purchase will be recorded on the scorecard in the time period in which the contract is signed.

It is generally much easier to critique an existing paragraph than to try to write it perfectly the first time. So now that the initial try has been made, the next two steps in the process are to review the list of questions to see if all have been answered, and modify the paragraph if needed. It is instructive to keep two key questions in mind when performing this paragraph review. The first is: "Does the paragraph make sense?" In other words, would everyone in your organization who needs to understand the interpretation of the measure read the definition the same way, or would there be ambiguity? The second key question is: "Is the definition what you want to use?" In other words, the definition might make perfectly logical sense, but you might be able to think of a much better way to define the measure.

The first question on the brainstorming list was: "What is a *new* customer?" According to the hastily written first-draft definition, a new customer is "any customer that is making their first purchase ever from our organization." Applying the two test questions, it might be concluded that this definition makes perfect logical sense, but there may be a better way to do it. For example, an insurance company might have large industrial property and casualty divisions. These are totally independent product lines with separate balance sheets and underwriters and so forth. They also go about customer acquisition separately. In other words, having a customer for casualty products doesn't necessarily make the client more attractive to the property division. If both divisions are responsible for finding new customers, the definition might need to be modified. It could be changed to:

> New customer dollars will be counted as those dollars received from any *product line* customer that is making their first purchase ever from *that product line*. The total dollar value of the purchase will be recorded on the scorecard in the time period in which the contract is signed.

The next question is: "How long will a customer be considered new for scorecard purposes?" The purpose of this question is to ensure that new customers are not counted as new customers forever; at some point they will become existing customers and no longer part of this measure. If the team feels that a 12-month period is sufficient before the customer will not be considered new any more (which makes sense if this were an insurance example since most premiums are paid and renewed annually), then this could be added as shown:

> New customer dollars will be counted as those dollars received from any product line customer that is making their first purchase ever from that product line. *Customers will be counted as new for twelve months following their initial product line purchase.* The total dollar value of the purchase will be recorded on the scorecard in the time period in which the contract is signed.

The third question asks: "Is there a statute of limitations?" According to the paragraph, there is not. The paragraph says that the customer must be making their first product line purchase *ever*. If the team reasons that a customer that bought from the company several years ago and stopped should now be considered a new customer, the paragraph would need to be modified again. It could be changed to read:

> New customer dollars will be counted as those dollars received from any product line customer that is making their first purchase *in the last five years* from that product line. Customers will be counted as new for twelve months following their initial product line purchase. The total dollar value of the purchase will be recorded on the scorecard in the time period in which the contract is signed.

The fourth question is: "Will the dollars be recorded on the BSC in the month the contract is signed or prorated over the life of the contract?" This question would be obvious if it were an insurance example, as premium is paid up front. No modifications to the definition would need to be made.

The final question is: "Is there a minimum dollar value to be considered for scorecarding purposes, or does any purchase by a customer count?" This question is designed to weed out small customers if the executive team wishes to do so. Perhaps only customers giving over $50,000 in business would be what the executive team wished to focus on. If this were the case, the final modification could be:

> New customer dollars will be counted as those dollars received from any product line customer that is making their first *large (> $50,000)* purchase in the last five years from that product line. Customers will be counted as new for twelve months following their initial product line purchase. The total dollar value of the purchase will be recorded on the scorecard in the time period in which the contract is signed.

This process of trial and error continues until the team has a definition they feel comfortable with. Some tips to aid in measurement definition are as follows:

- *Lists are helpful for clarification:* Lists can remove ambiguity. For example, if there is a measure of *training days per employee*, it is sometimes difficult for a team to precisely determine what counts as training and what does not. For instance, does night school count? What about on-the-job-training? Online training? And even if the team narrows the focus to "formal, in-classroom training with an instructor," potential definition problems still abound. Do the training classes have to be tied to subjects illustrated on the strategy map? And if so, who makes the determination of whether a class is relevant?

  A list can solve all of these problems. The team can make an accepted list of courses, and the ambiguity is gone. If an employee takes a course on the list, it counts as part of the measure. If the course is not on the list, it doesn't count. Case closed. Anti-lists are also helpful for clarification. This means saying "every formal training course counts *except . . .* " and making the list of excluded courses.

- *Don't use the word "etcetera"*: Using "etcetera" usually invalidates the definition. The lack of clarity introduced by the word leaves too much interpretation to the readers of the definition.

- *Determine an appropriate level of precision*: It is important for the team to determine how much precision is needed for the executive team to make sound business decisions. If it is enough for the executives to know that there were 3.1 training days per employee, for example, then don't set up a data collection procedure designed to deliver results to a 3.1428 level of accuracy. Making data collection as simple as possible is one of the keys to sustaining the scorecard over the long term.

- *Remember strategy map connections*: When defining a measure such as *training days per employee*, the team will have to decide what training will count. One factor in this decision should be the strategy map connections. The strategy map in the last chapter had an objective of *Develop High-Quality Staff*, which drove *Accelerate Product Development Time* and *Build Strong Customer Relationships*. The team may decide that the best way to achieve strategic success is to confine the training days to those courses that support product development and/or customer relationship building. (Again, this would be an excellent application of the listing technique.)

- *Avoid long, flowery, non-value-added statements*: The goal when writing a definition is to be direct, clear, and concise. Sometimes teams get into a mindset of "the more we write, the better off we'll be" or "we need to make every definition sound impressive, like it was written by a famous author." It is not uncommon to read the *training days per employee* definition and see a long-winded soliloquy like, "Training is part of the overall development plan for the workforce. Workforce development plans are an essential part of the organization's career development program, and contribute to the overall health and well-being of the organization."

This sounds great but really doesn't add any value to the definition. In fact, it can detract from definition quality if readers come to different conclusions regarding what the writers are trying to say. Readers will automatically think that they need to make some type of decision based on the wording, so they may come to inaccurate conclusions about what is being said.

As previously mentioned, writing a definition will take about an hour. This includes time to write and critique a definition paragraph, test it out with the experts who know the subject in question (these could be people not on the implementation team), and review the feedback with the team. Formalizing the definition by adding the data collection procedures and strategy map connections will add a marginal amount of time. So make sure to screen as many measures as possible before getting to this phase!

The next step in the measurement development process is to collect the data to fill in on the scorecard. Some of the barriers to successful data collection are as follows:

- *No data exists:* Scorecard measures often involve topics that have never been measured before. In this case the team must set up a data collection procedure from scratch, including designating a collector of the information. It is generally recommended that the team set up the procedure for presentation to the executive team, but not actually install the procedure until the executives formally approve the measure. (The approval process will be discussed shortly.)
- *Lack of systems:* Sometimes the data for a given measure already exist, but they are scattered throughout the organization and difficult to assemble. One facilitator found that the information needed to simply count the precise number of customers was in 26 separate databases. Sorting through all of them and editing out duplications took a team of people an entire week to finish. This can be

a minor issue or major complication, depending on the organization and what measures are being sought. The best solution is to be careful during measurement selection to try to avoid measures that will require horribly complex collection.

- *No discipline for data collection:* This is a common problem. When asking employees to be rigorous about data collection on topics that have never been measured before, there will almost always be start-up problems. Even if the employees in question are supportive of the process (which is certainly not a given), altering their established routine to include collecting new data will be difficult. The first thing the implementation needs to have is patience; the data collection people should be given the support needed to transition to new procedures. But it should be noted that the other thing the team needs is management support. If resistance to data collection becomes a persistent issue, then management will need to reemphasize the importance of the scorecard to those who are not complying with data collection requests.

- *Difficult to make the number meaningful in a one-number BSC format:* Sometimes the data collection process reveals that making the number meaningful in scorecard format isn't possible, even after a plausible definition has been created. Perhaps the definition suggests creating an index that sounds great initially, but upon further review is difficult to interpret meaningfully. This can happen when administering an employee survey, for example, and weighting each question to come up with an overall score of "86" for the scorecard. If it isn't apparent what 86 means or whether it is good or bad, the number really won't help that much.

- *Measure doesn't reveal anything useful:* If a team wanted to keep track of the number of new products, for example, they might write an excellent definition and assign the data collection to someone. This person might in turn realize that, the way the measure is defined, there will be at most one or two new products in any given year. This will turn the scorecard into a spectacularly uninteresting string of zeros, with an occasional 1 mixed in. And since the new product intros happen so infrequently, everybody knows about them anyway. This means there is no real reason to take up scorecard space with the number.

Navigating through these barriers can be time consuming and will almost certainly result in altering the format of the scorecard somewhat over the course of time. Initial efforts should be made to determine the difficulty of the data collection, but the team should present their recommendations to the leadership team before significant time is invested. This leadership team presentation is the final step of the measurement development process. The implementation team should prepare a document for the presentation that includes:

- *A "real" scorecard that has all the measures and easily gathered data already filled in.* The scorecard should be presented in the format recommended by the team. (In other words, if the team feels that "year-to-date" and "last month" columns are needed to tell the story properly, these should be presented as well.)
- *A "mock" scorecard that is completely filled in, including fictitious targets and comments.* It is difficult to get a feel for the complexity of a scorecard unless you can see what a completely finished product would look like. The "real" scorecard referenced in the prior point might be 50% blank due to data collection issues. This might make adding data columns sound like a good idea. But when all the blanks are filled in, it could be a different story. So the team should make up realistic numbers for all the measurement categories that don't have real data, and make up targets as well. Not only does this provide a good demo of what the finished product would look like, but comparing the mock scorecard to the real one gives the leadership team a good indication of how much work is left to be done.
- *A sample measurement definition.* Executives will probably not have the appetite for detail to go through each individual definition word for word, but it is a good idea to have a sample definition in the presentation package to illustrate the format and thinking that went into each measure.

- *A sample chart.* The control charts referenced in the assessment section are excellent tools to aid in providing context to the scorecard measures. Other charts and graphs may be used to help aid in interpretation as well. Including a sample chart as a demo can be instructive for the leadership team.
- *Appendices containing the remainder of the definitions and charts.* It is important to have all the detail handy to answer any questions that may arise.

The meeting to discuss the implementation team recommendations can easily last half a day. The premeeting process of creating and debating the definitions usually results in the team being well-prepared to answer any questions the executives throw at them. This makes the team sound intelligent and thorough, which is confidence-inspiring for the executives.

The team should *not* be intimidated or have their feelings hurt if and when the leaders challenge their recommendations. On the contrary; if the leaders accepted the recommendations wholesale, then it would be more of a concern. Unless the implementation team is extraordinarily good and lucky, they won't deliver the perfect set of measures on the first try. Complete acceptance of the measures with no push back could imply the leadership isn't really taking the BSC seriously. The executives might question a particular measure's relevance or ask, "why not B versus A?" The job of the implementation team is to forcefully present the reasoning behind the choice of each measure—once. If the executives persist in wanting to drop or change a measure, then the implementation team should cheerfully go along. It is important to remember that the customer of the scorecard is the leadership; the job is to give them a product they want and will use.

It is inevitable that the leaders will want scorecard modifications, so the team will need to continue to define and collect until a complete set of measures has been agreed upon. At this juncture, the leaders will be responsible for target setting and initiative selection. These functions should not be viewed as independent events. If an aggressive target is set, then aggressive initiatives need to be implemented to back it up. Success with an initiative should drive positive results with the scorecard measures. Some tips for target setting are as follows:

- *Remember to use the strategy map:* It has been stated that targets are often pulled out of thin air. The strategy map chapter illustrated how to use the map to make target setting a bit more logical. Start at the top with the number-one measure and decide what the target should be. Then use the connections throughout the rest of the diagram to set supporting targets that drive the desired numbers at the top.

- *Remember that targets don't come free:* If a target is set with no means identified for execution, it implies that all people have to do is try harder to achieve it. In the vast majority of cases, this will not be effective. The executive team is accountable for resource allocation to drive the achievement of targets. Once the number is set, the executives should immediately think about the "how" of making it happen.

- *Decide what happens if a target is made or missed:* The executives should make it clear who is primarily responsible for achieving each target and what the process is going to be if the target is achieved (or not). An acceptable answer to this question is "nothing," if that is what the leadership team wants. But if it doesn't make any difference whether a target is made, then why bother setting one in the first place? Usually there should be something at stake, be it compensation, recognition, or promotion. It should also be determined whether compensation rules regarding targets are hard and fast. Remember that when an organization has used a scorecard for a while, it generally progresses to the level of analyzing *why* the target was missed. If it was missed due to a manager's inattention to a strategic initiative, for example, the compensation ramifications might need to be different than if a target was missed due to a factor beyond the manager's control.

Once the targets are set, the scorecard will be ready for use. It is important to remember, however, that the scorecard is simply an information-providing tool. A good analogy is to view the scorecard like a scale when you are on a diet. Stepping on a scale does not make you weigh less (unless you fiddle with the knobs!); the function of the scale is simply to tell you how you are doing. The scorecard is the same way. An organization shouldn't expect to get better just because they are stepping on a strategic scale every so often. In the same way that changing eating habits, establishing an exercise routine, and so on make the diet successful, execution of strategic initiatives makes a strategy successful. The next section provides insights into the identification and prioritization of strategic initiatives.

STRATEGIC INITIATIVES: IMPLEMENTATION

The identification and prioritization of initiatives is a critical step in the process because it establishes what will actually get done. This step is the primary responsibility of the *executive team*. The process is fairly straightforward, with the steps illustrated in Exhibit 5.13.

EXHIBIT 5.13   *Initiative Identification and Prioritization Process*

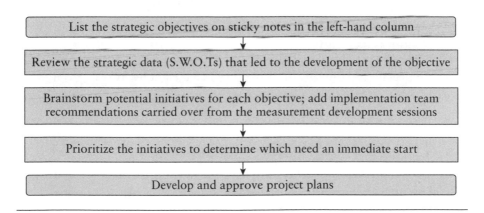

The first step involves creating a template as shown in Exhibit 5.14, with the objectives on the left being in a column of sticky notes on the wall or whiteboard.

The next step is to review the strategic data (S.W.O.Ts) that led to the development of the objective. Many of the items that were brainstormed as opportunities could be ready-made initiatives. Weaknesses and threats might suggest potential initiatives that would close gaps, and strengths might suggest initiatives that would help leverage excellent performance. In all cases, it is important to refresh the executive team's memory on the strategic issues.

The next step is simply to brainstorm potential initiatives for each objective. The team should not restrict their thinking to only those things the organization would rush right out and do *tomorrow*; anything is fair game at this point. The team should supplement their brainstorming list by adding the implementation team recommendations carried over from the measurement development session. As each idea is surfaced, it should be written on a sticky note and placed in the "Potential Initiatives" column of the template in the row of the objective it corresponds to. For example, the *Develop High-Quality Staff* objective could look as shown in Exhibit 5.15.

Once potential initiatives for *all* objectives have been identified and listed, the executive team needs to prioritize them to determine which need an immediate start. The reason the template is divided into three numerical columns is to illustrate relative priority. The definition of each column is as follows:

- 1 = urgent and important; must be started right away (i.e., do it *now*)
- 2 = important, but not urgent; (i.e., do it *soon*)
- 3 = interesting, but not an immediate priority (i.e., do it when you get around to it)

It is *extremely important* that this be viewed on a cross-objective basis. In other words, don't brainstorm potential initiatives for each objective and rank them individually within each objective. Instead, brainstorm initiatives for *all* the objectives first, and *then* decide what

EXHIBIT **5.14**   *Strategic Initiative Template*

Strategic Objectives	1	2	3	Potential Initiatives
Financial • Maximize profitability • Increase revenue • Reduce costs				
Customer • Build strong customer relationships • Penetrate new markets • Maintain top reputation				
Processes • Increase on-time delivery % • Accelerate product development time • Optimize supply chain				
Learning and Growth • Develop high-quality staff • Improve internal comm. • Upgrade systems				

the top-priority initiatives from the entire list should be. The reason for this is that "customer service training" might look like a number-one priority when compared only to the other potential initiatives in the list for *Develop High-Quality Staff*, but when compared to potential initiatives from all the other objectives, it clearly might not be an area that needs immediate attention.

EXHIBIT 5.15 *Strategic Initiatives Example*

Strategic Objectives	1	2	3	Potential Initiatives
Develop high-quality staff				• Benefit review
				• Hiring process analysis
				• Initiate career development program
				• Succession planning process analysis
				• Gainsharing
				• Customer service training
				• 7 hats of creative thinking training
				• Individual training plan development

As the leadership team determines what the priority of each initiative should be, the sticky note containing the objective should be removed from the *Potential Initiatives* column and placed in the properly numbered column. It is common for the leaders to start by ranking far too many initiatives in the top-priority column. This brings up a very important question: How many "1's" can you have?

There are two important considerations when answering this question. The first considers the nature of the initiatives. It might be logically impossible for initiative B to begin before initiative A ends, because it may be dependent upon the results. The other consideration is cost. Every initiative comes with a cost: people, time, investment in improvement ideas, and the like. The executives have to balance how much time, effort, and money can be funneled into strategic work without damaging the performance of day-to-day functions. This can be very difficult to do. So the answer to the number of top-priority initiatives that can be started simultaneously is as many as you can afford—as long as the initiatives aren't dependent on each other for success. When the top-priority initiatives have all been identified, the last step in the process is to develop project plans that nail down the specifics of execution.

BALANCED SCORECARD UTILIZATION

The scorecard, strategy map, and initiative list should all be used together when the management team is discussing strategy. The scorecard will identify the areas in which the targets are not being met, and the strategy map and list of initiatives can provide clues to the leadership team as to why this may be happening. A predicted relationship among objectives may not exist. For example, the leadership team might have thought training would lead to product development cycle time reduction, but after everyone in the area received training, the cycle time was unaffected. This means that either the connection on the strategy map was inaccurate or the training was ineffective. If the training was ineffective, it could have been because of the delivery or because the employees were incapable of learning the needed skills.

This point is very important. The tools will tell the management team *what* is going on, but *they* must determine *why* it is happening. The tools can provide clues, but the managers have to know their business well enough to act on the clues and solve the problem correctly. A speaker at a convention once told a story about starting a basketball team. She said that if you were starting a team, you could teach someone how to dribble better and you could teach someone to pass better, but you couldn't teach someone to be *tall*. A player is either tall or not tall, and that is a characteristic present from the time they all walk on the court. She went on to say that in many organizations there are some very short people who are trying to play in the NBA. In other words, people who are overmatched by the job responsibilities they have been given. And this doesn't mean they haven't been trained; it means that they simply don't have what it takes to be successful in the position in which they have been placed.

The scorecard and strategy map are both great tools. If you give great tools to good managers, they become great managers. If you give great tools to bad managers, they remain bad managers—but with tools. The scorecard simply gives bad managers another thing to mismanage. So if your leadership team doesn't truly understand your customers and processes and people, the BSC and strategy map won't help you very much. However, if you have a strong team already, these tools can help position your organization for true short- and long-term success.

CHAPTER 6

CONCLUSIONS

The key points are as follows:

- Current trends in the business world are forcing organizations to focus on process if they want to remain successful. Many of these trends, such as the mobility of the workforce, rising customer expectations, and the speed at which business is conducted, are not likely to stop in the near future. Therefore, process emphasis will continue to grow as a key component of future organizational success.
- Companies have elevated process thinking to higher and higher levels over the years. From continuous improvement to reengineering to process-based organizational design to process-based competition, the emphasis on process excellence has become an integral part of management thinking and planning in successful organizations.
- A good vision statement enables an organization to have a consistent view of what it wants the future to look like. It is impossible to reach the desired future state if the management team cannot agree what the future state should be.
- Strategic assessment should have a large process component to it. Gone are the days when the focus of planning can be purely financial. Strategies of today must also include the process, customer, and learning and growth components.
- Strategy maps can provide an excellent one-page communication vehicle to illustrate which processes are most critical in your

organization, as well as the customer and financial results that improving these processes are expected to drive.

- The Balanced Scorecard is an excellent tool to help an organization monitor the effectiveness of strategy and make midterm course corrections between iterations of the strategic planning process. It also helps reveal whether the strategy map theories of cause and effect are valid, which is extremely useful when trying to understand the impact of improving key processes.

The techniques and processes introduced have been proven time and again to be effective when properly applied. Good luck with your implementation of these principles. Here's hoping that the *fifth* wave of process management will be a result of *your* efforts.

INDEX